LOST
TOWNS OF MONROE COUNTY,
MICHIGAN

···

Shawna Lynn Mazur

THE
History
PRESS

Published by The History Press
Charleston, SC
www.historypress.com

First published 2024

Manufactured in the United States

ISBN 9781467157926

Library of Congress Control Number: 2024937592

Notice: The information in this book is true and complete to the best of our knowledge. It is offered without guarantee on the part of the author or The History Press. The author and The History Press disclaim all liability in connection with the use of this book.

This book is dedicated to my husband, Joseph Mazur, who has helped me every step of the way in this project—and in my life, too! Also, to my father, David Grosse, who passed away in 2023 and encouraged me to write this second book; I am just sorry he won't be able to see the finished product. And to my son, Tyler Mazur, who shares my love of history and writing, too! I hope his son, Harrison, born in 2023, will share in our passion, too!

CONTENTS

PREFACE

I am privileged to be able to say I was born in Monroe and have spent my whole life in Monroe County. Monroe is steeped in so much history, and the more you dig, the more you find. When I wrote *Hidden History of Monroe County, Michigan* (2022), I found that volumes upon volumes could be written about Monroe. Yet there are so few books about Monroe. Luckily, we have two definitive history books compiled at the beginning of the twentieth century, written by John Bulkley and Talcott Wing.

I had the idea to write this book after writing *Hidden History of Monroe County, Michigan*, in which I featured a few lost towns. I initially wondered if such a book could be written about Monroe County's lost towns. After all, how many towns could there possibly have been? I theorized that if I came upon thirty or so, I could write the book. Little did I know what I was in for when I discovered over one hundred! How could Monroe County have so many lost towns? This book became a real labor of love, and I poured countless hours into research, map analyzing, traveling all over the county multiple times and putting it all together. It took well over two years.

But I must say, it was a real pleasure learning about all the towns and areas Monroe once had and, especially, learning about life back then. We can learn so much about our present by looking at our past and appreciating how hard it was for our ancestors to live—so we could be here today. You might find in any given town that you had an ancestor there. From those who founded a village to those who started up thriving industries or stores and who farmed or cared for the homestead: each person in some way contributed to the community. The old saying "Everyone knew everyone" was never so true as back then. The communities were tight-knit, and everyone depended on each other, sometimes even for survival.

My purpose in writing this book was to highlight Monroe County's history in a definitive book that covers all the different towns and the like that existed: how, why and where they came to be, what life was like then, who lived there and what happened to them.

I wanted to write a book that would give readers a glimpse into life in early Monroe, as well as some key aspects of its community and historical significance. We have the advantage of looking back over 240 years. I hope that this narrative will inspire others to appreciate the history of this fascinating county and want to dig more themselves. By doing so, we learn more about those who lived here, those who struggled here and all those who made sacrifices for us to be here today.

ACKNOWLEDGEMENTS

I am indebted to many individuals in writing this book, as well as many historical sources and institutions. I would like to thank the Monroe County Library System (MCLS), the *Monroe News*, the River Raisin National Battlefield Park, the Monroe County Historical Society, the Monroe County Genealogical Society, the Milan Public Library and the Monroe County Museum System.

I want to express my gratitude to the following individuals:

John Rodrigue, acquisitions editor, The History Press

Zoe Ames, copyeditor, The History Press

Joseph Mazur

Tyler Mazur

David Grosse

Regina Manning, Monroe County Library System, Ellis Reference and Information Center reference librarian

Charmaine Wawrzyniec, Monroe County Library System, Ellis Reference and Information Center, curator of the Lawrence A. Frost Collection of Custeriana

Lou Komorowski, Monroe County Library System, Ellis Reference and Information Center reference manager

Marian Sisung, thank you for sharing your history, knowledge and photos of Grape.

Suzanne Krueger, community librarian, Ida Branch, Monroe County Library System

Adrian Childress, reference librarian, Bedford Branch, Monroe County Library System

Sarah Dauvignon, reference librarian, Milan Public Library

Barbara Beaton, assistant director, Milan Public Library

Shannen McMahon, community librarian, Erie and Luna Pier Branches, Monroe County Library System

Jennifer Grudnoski, Dundee area supervisor, Dundee, Maybee, Summerfield-Petersburg, Monroe County Library System

Russell Davis, author and historian

Ralph Naveaux, author and historian

David Ingall, author and historian

INTRODUCTION

Officially, Monroe County was carved out of the southernmost area of Wayne County in 1817. Michigan was not a state yet and was part of the Old Northwest Territory. Situated in the southeasterly corner of Michigan, Monroe County covers an area of about 542 square miles and has fifteen counties. The River Raisin cuts a swath 139 miles from Hillsdale County through the entire county of Monroe until it dumps into Lake Erie. Lake Erie, the shallowest of the Great Lakes, borders the county to the east. The River Raisin and Lake Erie are the features that drew settlers to the area and helped to develop communities that relied on water for sustenance. Today, people are still drawn to Monroe's scenic river views, sandy beaches and eclectic mix of urban and rural areas.

We are going to travel back in time and visit Monroe County's lost towns. Just what does the phrase *lost town* mean? In fact, that is a hard thing to pin down. Often towns had a school, a church, a general store and perhaps a post office. If the town had a post office, it knew it had made it! But sometimes "towns" were not officially designated towns at all but places that sprang up to fulfill a need. We are not going to make a hard and fast definition here but rather look at places that existed in one way or the other. For example, some towns were full-fledged communities; others were just a railroad or stagecoach stop. Some still exist, if only as shadows of their former selves. Others have been lost entirely, leaving no clue they ever existed.

Lost towns did not just appear haphazardly. Usually, at least one of three things had to be present for a lost town to develop: a major road, a railroad or a waterway. As you read about these areas, you will see that most did indeed have a railroad. And when the railroad passenger service disappeared, so did the towns.

For much of the 1800s, most settlements in Monroe County developed around waterways and/or thoroughfares, which usually began as Native American trails. In the late 1800s, in Monroe County, when most towns boomed, the railroads were going through. Many of the towns we look at in this book reached their heyday at the beginning of the twentieth century. By the first quarter of the twentieth century, they were on their way out as the railroads disappeared and the automobile took over. The automobile was the death knell of most of these towns.

If any remnants of these lost towns survive, they usually consist of a schoolhouse, a church, a cemetery and a few houses. If the schoolhouse still exists, it has often been repurposed as a residence or the like. Please remember that such sites are private property now and be respectful of the owners. As far as the churches go, most belong to a different denomination now. Many of the cemeteries still exist, but there are some entirely forgotten and under houses, stores, and so on.

Information about lost towns can be very scant; sometimes, the name of a town just appears in a newspaper or on a map. I had to consult multiple sources to try and find anything and everything I possibly could. Maps are the key to tracking down these towns: the years they appear and disappear, as well as what was in the town itself. I pored over more than one hundred maps of Monroe County. You will see references to multiple maps in this book, but in particular four of them, which I encourage you to consult throughout the narrative. These are available online, and I have provided the links to them here as well as further information about them in the bibliography:

The 1859 Geil map:
https://www.loc.gov/item/2012593018/

The 1901 Lang map:
https://www.loc.gov/item/2012593017/

The 1876 Beers atlas:
https://quod.lib.umich.edu/m/micounty/3927905.0001.001/5

The 1896 Ogle atlas:
https://quod.lib.umich.edu/m/micounty/3927818.0001.001

Unbelievably, Monroe has more than one hundred lost towns and the like across its fifteen townships! Each town has surprises to reveal about what life was like in the way of industry operations, merchants, farming, schooling, activities, crime, mysteries, Prohibition, tragedies, epidemics, etc. Learn about the town developed by a murderer, a town where the mayor runs everything, paper towns and wildcat banks, bank robberies and more.

Discover how many towns were founded by a family patriarch and named after him. Could your ancestor be one of them? Why were the towns located where they were, how did they develop and why did they disappear without a trace? Why were three bustling villages lost not only to Monroe but also to the state of Michigan? Believe it or not, Monroe has its own Atlantis story. Many of the cemeteries associated with these towns disappeared just like they did; could your property be on one of them? What was life like in the nineteenth and twentieth centuries? What did Henry Ford have to do with any of these towns? Are there any traces of the towns today?

Monroe County, Michiga

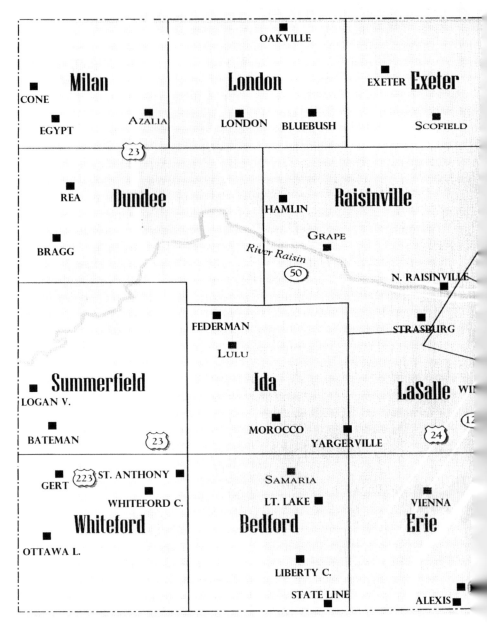

OAKVILLE

Milan

CONE

EGYPT

AZALIA

London

LONDON   BLUEBUSH

EXETER **Exeter**

SCOFIELD

23

REA   **Dundee**

BRAGG

HAMLIN

GRAPE

River Raisin

50

Raisinville

N. RAISINVILLE

FEDERMAN

LULU

STRASBURG

Summerfield

LOGAN V.

BATEMAN   23

Ida

MOROCCO

YARGERVILLE

LaSalle WI

24   12

GERT   223 ST. ANTHONY

WHITEFORD C.

Whiteford

OTTAWA L.

SAMARIA

LT. LAKE

Bedford

LIBERTY C.

STATE LINE

VIENNA

Erie

ALEXIS

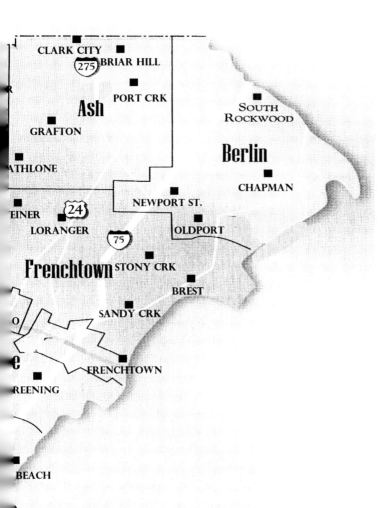

Map of Monroe County, Michigan. Lost town notations by author. *Monroe Publishing Company*

Chapter 1

TOWNSHIP DEVELOPMENT

C ongress authorized the governor General Lewis Cass to organize the Michigan territory into townships on February 25, 1825. In Monroe County, in 1827, five townships were organized: Monroe, Frenchtown, Raisinville, Erie and Port Lawrence.

Since the territory was largely unsettled, the townships encompassed large amounts of land. It was not until 1848 that the City of Monroe was actually set off by itself from Monroe Township. Frenchtown was the largest of the townships and included the original settlement by the same name. Erie had the distinction of being the first township settled in the county, named after Lake Erie. Raisinville was named after the River Raisin and was very large to start, but later, Ida, London, Summerfield, Milan and Dundee would all be sliced out of it. Port Lawrence ended up in the disputed territory of the 1836 Toledo War and eventually was lost to Ohio, becoming part of Lucas County.

OTHER TOWNSHIPS

We are going to look at lost towns in each township, but first, we need to look at the development of the township itself.

Ash was carved out of Frenchtown Township in 1837 and named after Arba Ash.

Bedford was originally part of Erie Township and was called West Erie at first. The town of Bedford was organized in 1836 and named after New York City.

Berlin was organized in 1867 out of Ash Township and named after Berlin, Germany.

Dundee was organized out of Summerfield and Raisinville Townships in 1838. It was named after Dundee, Scotland.

Exeter, founded 1836, was originally part of Raisinville and named after the birthplace of its first supervisor. London developed out of the township in 1832 and was named after London, England.

Ida was organized out of Raisinville, Dundee and Summerfield in 1837. It was named after schoolteacher Ida M. Taylor.

Lasalle was one of the earliest settlements, with twenty-two families, in 1794; it was organized into a township in 1830 from part of Erie. LaSalle was named after a Mr. Lasalle, who operated a store there; it was also called the Otter Creek Settlement.

Milan was organized in 1836 by carving out a piece of London Township and was named after Milan, Italy.

Summerfield was organized in 1829 and used to be called Flumen.

Whiteford was in Port Lawrence and Erie and then organized to be its own township in 1834. It was named after General David White.

Chapter 2

A SLICE OF LIFE

Roads

When reading through interviews, stories and accounts of people who lived in these towns, I found that many of them repeat the same scenarios over and over and have a lot in common. Most of the stories talk about the horrible conditions of the roads, which were nothing more than heaps of mud. This hindered transportation on a grand scale. Horses struggled to pull carriages through the muddy mess. Often people were forced to simply walk miles at a time, especially to school. Stories of walking to school for miles in every kind of weather are common.

The original roads were usually Native American trails or corduroy roads. A corduroy road was built of logs where it forded streams, swamps and the like; otherwise, it was just dirt. The largest was Hull's Road, a military road, which followed a Native American trail that ran north to south. This road was well traversed not only by the army but also by many a traveler, as it ran from Detroit to Dayton, Ohio. Multiple coaches traversed its length on a daily basis up until the advent of the railroads. As early as 1836, there was a stagecoach line between Monroe and Ann Arbor that was utilized constantly. Like many stops we imagine in old western towns, Monroe had its share of taverns and saloons in almost every village that popped up along the roadways. Journeys were long and arduous, and everyone looked forward to a stagecoach stop where they could rest their weary bones. Even the horses

A load of lager at Martin's Place Saloon, Newport, 1912. *Monroe Publishing Company.*

needed a respite. Taverns and saloons catered to the wants of the patrons with down-home cooked meals, restful beds, music, dancing and plenty of libations to raise the weary spirit.

RAILROADS

Later, with the advent of the railroad, residents knew that settlements needed to be by the railroad route to succeed. Sometimes, settlements formed in anticipation of the railroad coming through. If it did not for some reason, the residents knew it was all over, and in a few cases, they even gathered up their homes and businesses and moved.

More than anything else, railroads are what created towns. The Erie & Kalamazoo was the first railroad west of the Allegheny River to run through Monroe County, in 1836. There were depots in almost every town where there were two tracks crossing. In 1910, Monroe County was crisscrossed with railroads and had thirty-three depots serving the Ann Arbor, Detroit and Toledo Shoreline, Detroit, Monroe and Toledo Shortline, Detroit, Toledo and Ironton, Lake Shore and Michigan Southern, Michigan Central and Pierre Marquette Railroads. Passenger service brought people to the areas and then necessitated lodging, food,

Gas train arriving at Azalia Depot, 1911. *Milan Public Library.*

and on and on. The industry also brought people by train to settle and work in the towns.

But once the automobile came along, the railroad cars no longer carried passengers and basically became freight trains; thus, the towns started drying up. So when the railroads disappeared, so did the towns.

Industry/Business

Industry played a large part in the development of a town: there had to be a way to sustain a living. Gristmills, sawmills, quarries, and all kinds of factories—from cider, sorghum, pickle, beet, cheese, tomato canning and hoop and stave factories—dotted the landscape. Lime kilns, charcoal kilns and brick and tile kilns were everywhere. Limestone from quarries was used in building foundations, while lime was used for the glue to hold them together as well as to plaster walls. Wood was used to build homes and businesses as well as for heat. Charcoal was used for heat and kerosene, and candles were used for light. Because of all this, structure fires were fairly common.

Mercantile businesses were also everywhere: general stores, butcher shops, icehouses, blacksmith shops, hotels, taverns, carriage makers, barbers, hardware stores, and more.

Gesell General Store, Monroe, 1918. *Monroe County Library System, Ellis.*

Many towns had railroad depots, schools, multiple churches, cemeteries, banks and, if they were lucky, their own post office.

SETTLERS

In the 1800s, many settlers were looking to move west from the East Coast in hopes of building a better future for themselves. Many came from New York. They would buy up as much land as they could afford. The going rate for land was $1.25 an acre, and the land office of Monroe only required a $100 deposit. They traveled in Conestoga wagons to get to their promised land and, on arrival, realized that they had a lot of work ahead of them. Most of the land had to be cleared before they could even build a cabin. Many German immigrants preferred the land that was already cleared, as they did not have to worry about logging but could go straight to farming.

Most settlers were farmers, and agriculture was the mainstay of their occupation. Farming was very arduous, requiring crude implements and plenty of horses and men. At the turn of the nineteenth century, steam engine tractors entered the picture, but those who had them were few and far between. They were very heavy, large and expensive.

Steam tractor, Ida. *Monroe County Library System, Ida.*

Life was not easy on the farm, with work to be done day and night. Many of the farmers looked to making additional income by selling their crops to gristmills, timber to lumber mills, milk to cheese factories, etc. Some even opened their own stores or started up an industry but still managed to keep up their farms. Their sons would help on the farm and were kept out of school during harvest season and the like. On top of schooling, they had to do their daily chores.

The women and daughters had to keep up the homestead and grow gardens, cook from scratch, take care of the animals, take care of the children, make their own clothes, do laundry, clean, etc. Life in the 1800s could be brutal.

SCHOOLS

The first one-room schoolhouses were usually built of wood and later rebuilt with brick. They had two windows on each side, a cedar-shingled roof, whitewashed walls and a painted black slate chalkboard. They were very small, fifteen by twenty feet, and were heated by woodstoves (some coal) located in the center of the building. Not surprisingly, many caught fire. Some teachers went in early by horse and buggy and heated up the stove before school started. The teacher's desk was usually elevated on a platform in front of the room. The students' desks consisted of rows, sometimes

Top: Fryburg School, London Township. *Milan Public Library.*

Bottom: Mardi Gras, Azalia. *Milan Public Library.*

attached to the walls. The grades were from kindergarten through eighth grade, ages three to eighteen years, with each school handling fifteen to twenty pupils. Water was collected from a well, and a pail was passed around for everyone to drink out of. Sometimes each pupil had their own cup; other times, they had to share a ladle. There were outhouses located outside, as well as a woodshed for storing wood or doling out discipline, if needed.

By 1860, there were seventy-five or more schools in the county. A new law was passed that stated no child under ten years old should be required to walk more than two miles one way to school. Larger schools started being built, with three windows on each side and two entrance doors to separate the male and female pupils. At the turn of the nineteenth century, even larger schools were built that had two classrooms atop an elevated basement area. In 1946, there were 144 schools, but by the late 1940s, most schools had consolidated into the public school districts of Monroe County.

Chapter 3

ASH TOWNSHIP

Athlone was a settlement in the 1840s, that grew up around a German Catholic community at Labo and Exeter Roads. St. Patrick's Church was originally a log house owned by James Donohoe in 1834. The actual church building was constructed in 1847 out of logs and was rebuilt out of bricks in 1861.

According to the St. Patrick's Church historical marker:

> *Irish and German immigrants first came to this area, known as Stony Creek, in the 1840s. The settlement was also called Athlone, after a city significant in Ireland's military history. Redemptorist missionaries served Catholics here from 1847 until 1855. On March 17, 1847, they celebrated the dedicatory Mass of their first church, which was built of logs donated by parishioners. On June 26, 1860, the cornerstone was laid for the present church; six months later the church was completed. Built in the Round-Arch mode, it once had a lofty spire surrounded by finials. On December 27, Bishop LeFevre appointed Father Desiderius Callaert the first resident pastor of Stony Creek, and St. Patrick's gained the full status of a parish.*

There were three cemeteries at St. Patrick's, with the first one being the oldest, located directly across from the church at Exeter and Labo Roads.

St. Patrick's Church, Athlone (modern-day Carleton). *Monroe County Library System, Ellis.*

A post office was opened on March 28, 1856, and ran until January 30, 1858. At first, it was in the home of one Mr. Berkhover, which was located on Exeter Road just a few hundred feet north of the church. The mail was brought in from Carleton and then disseminated. The post office reopened on December 29, 1863, and ran for a long time thereafter, until July 18, 1894.

The hamlet had about one hundred residents and a few stores. It was populated until about 1890, when people started to move closer to Carleton and Waltz.

St. Patrick's School was started by Father Smulders and, in 1848, housed in the log church. In 1867, a school, which also contained a convent, was built. In 1909, a separate convent building and a separate school building were constructed. However, on May 30, 1926, the school burned down. It was rebuilt on the same foundation right afterward and is the elementary school in Carleton today. In 1955, a second school building was built for the older grades.

Today, only the St. Patrick's Church complex, school and cemeteries still exist, as well as a few houses. Athlone appears on an 1873 and a 1909 map.

BRIAR HILL

Founded in the 1860s, Briar Hill grew up alongside the railroad station for the Detroit, Toledo & Ironton (DT&I) Railroad at what became known as Briar Hill Road. The hamlet, of about three hundred people, was founded by William Walters and was between Carleton and Flat Rock. Walters owned and operated numerous charcoal factories (some accounts say up to fifteen) that stretched from the railroad on either side for half a mile. He employed many workers to run the large, twelve-foot-wide kilns. Charcoal wagons were used to carry the charcoal, and they had six- to seven-foot-high sides. There was also a general store on the southwest corner of the railroad tracks and Briar Hill Road, as well as a sawmill.

Along the railroad tracks can be seen the cement foundations that Henry Ford had built. Henry Ford purchased the DT&I Railroad in 1920. He decided to experiment with an electrical railway, and around 1926, he electrified the railway route for about forty miles from the River Rouge to Flat Rock. He planned to continue the route westerly through Monroe County, passing right through Briar Hill. In Dearborn, the catenaries

Briar Hill former town area today. *Author.*

Briar Hill railroad tracks with foundations today. *Author.*

(arches) can be seen for the electric line, but in Monroe County he never got that far; he had the cement foundations put in for the catenaries, but they were never built. (See Diann under Dundee Township for more information.) He did, however, stop passenger transportation when he bought the railroad.

Briar Hill boomed in the 1860s and '70s. By 1890, it was more profitable for the workers to go work in Carleton or Waltz, and they started moving out. By 1900, all that was left was the store and some farms. The factories were just abandoned, so the farmers used the wood from them to their advantage.

There was a family cemetery, the Rubert Cemetery, on the east side of Briar Hill Road between Newburg and Carter Roads. There are no longer any remnants of the cemetery. As far as that goes, there are no longer any signs of the settlement either, other than the road that bears it name. It appears on a 1911 (Rand McNally) map and a 1930 map.

Clark City

John W. Clark moved his family from New York to Ash Township in 1854. He built a stave mill on Swan Creek, and soon the area was booming. A year later, a post office went up, on January 25, 1855; it ran until December 19, 1866, with Justus Clark as the first postmaster. A railroad was planned to go right through the area, which prompted many more people and businesses to settle there. Before long, it had over two hundred residents, a jewelry store, a cigar shop, a blacksmith shop, a carriage shop, a brickyard, two churches, a hotel, a school, a library, a dentist's office and numerous stores.

The school located at Swan Creek and Labo Roads was called Labo School before 1907, then became Clark. It is in the 1876 Beers atlas, and it was rebuilt in 1896 and stayed at the same location until it closed in 1948.

But as was often the case, the railroad changed its plans and decided to locate elsewhere and left the settlement high and dry. The residents knew they were doomed and decided to abandon the little city, but not without trying to move as many buildings as they could on sleds over the ice in the winter. All traces of the town were gone by 1877, except the cemetery, which was all but forgotten.

Today, the cemetery is on private property. It intersects Will-Carleton Road and I-275 and is now completely surrounded by industry, as is the area that once was Clark City. There was a rumor that when I-275 was being constructed, the workers came across the cemetery and saw that a Civil War veteran was buried there. Unfortunately, they disturbed the grave by digging it up in hopes of finding a Civil War–era relic. When the foreman discovered what they were up to, he put an abrupt stop to it. Yet four years later, cemetery volunteers discovered the grave had sunk to a depth of four feet or so. Clark City appears on the 1859 Geil map.

Grafton

Grafton still exists today, mostly as a road in Ash Township. Josiah Littlefield, from Grafton, New York, founded the settlement in 1835 and named it after his hometown. Grafton grew up along a railroad line and became the station for the Pierre Marquette Railroad. A post office was established on March 14, 1850, and ran until April 30, 1903, with Littlefield as the first postmaster. Littlefield established a store at the northeast corner of Grafton and Sigler Roads. His store ledger still survives and has account

Grafton former town area today. *Author.*

after account of bartering in it, showing how Littlefield was more than generous in helping out his neighbors during hard times. He often let their bills ride and never collected the debt. The post office and railroad station were also located in this vicinity. The store supposedly witnessed a murder sometime in its history.

The community eventually had a business district, stores, a sawmill, a blacksmith shop and a Methodist church. In 1840, the Littlefield family donated land to build the Grafton School at the northeast corner of Grafton and Sigler Roads. A new school was built on the same site in 1915. The morning of January 23, 1931, would not soon be forgotten by the pupils and teacher at the school. Suddenly, the furnace exploded, and a large plume of fire illuminated the classroom. The substitute teacher, Mrs. Trent Cole, acted quickly and was able to put the fire out before anyone was injured. Oddly enough, the night before, about one ton of coal had been stolen from the schoolhouse. After the fire, the school was rebuilt again and, in 1948, became part of the Airport School District and was torn down.

The Grafton Mills were a mainstay in the community and were eventually purchased by Thomas Bodell, who came to the area in 1845; he ran the mills for five years. Another notable resident was Josiah's son, Levi

Grafton Cemetery today. *Author.*

B. Littlefield, who was a merchant and farmer at Grafton after serving as Ash Township supervisor for five years. He came to the township with his parents in 1835.

On Sigler Road, just west of Grafton Road, the Grafton Cemetery was established, although the year is not known. According to the 1859 Geil map, "R. Littlefield" owned the property, but in the 1896 George Olge atlas and on the 1901 Lang map, the property owner is Patrick Sims. In any case, many Littlefields are buried there. Today, the cemetery is surrounded by farmland and has a long, narrow lane leading to it, but the bridge can only be crossed by foot. Incidentally, there is a "no trespassing" sign posted, so permission needs to be granted first. Today, all that remains of Grafton is the cemetery. Grafton appears in the Beers atlas from 1876 and on other Monroe County maps until 1967.

Hicksville

Hicksville was proposed by David B. Hicks in 1836 as a village in section number 23 in Ash Township. It would be around the intersection of Telegraph and Sigler Roads on Swan Creek. Hicks proposed a sawmill and a millrace as part of the village. According to the 1859 Geil map, there was a church and school located there. The school was the Ash Center School, which was built in 1850 at Telegraph and Sigler Roads. It was moved in 1876 and eventually burned down. It does not appear that the proposed village ever became a reality, however. It is in the Monroe County deeds book.

Port Creek

Little is known about Port Creek except that there still exists a road named after the settlement. The actual creek ran into the Huron River. Port Creek used to be called "Pork Creek" because of all the wild hogs that made it their home. A church, a cemetery and a school were established on Port Creek Road. The cemetery, founded in 1834, is still there today and is also known as Evergreen. The school existed from 1878 to 1910, when a second, brick schoolhouse was built that lasted until it merged with the Airport School

Former Port Creek School, built in 1910. *Author.*

Port Creek Cemetery, established circa 1834. *Author.*

District in 1967. Today, the school has been converted into a house and is still located next to the cemetery.

The 1901 Lang map was created by George Earl Lang, Monroe County's famous cartographer. His grandparents were early settlers of Port Creek. George was born on October 8, 1873, in Ash Township, not far from Port Creek. In his twenties, he moved to Detroit, and in 1896, he came back to Monroe County and rode his bicycle around the entire county, which resulted in a published map of Monroe County, Michigan, in 1901 (which has been invaluable to this book). Unfortunately, much of his research was lost when his photography studio caught fire in 1916. Yet in 1917, he managed to publish *Pocket Road Map of Monroe County, Michigan: Monroe County Historical Data and Facts about Monroe County, Briefly Told*. In it, he writes: "Railroad facilities are unsurpassed, located between two great cities, telephone service, electricity, automobiles, good towns linked up with good roads, her chief city growing with leaps and bounds, with optimism in the air, it will be Monroe County and City First and Always." Later, he was village clerk and treasurer of Carleton. He also served as secretary of the Monroe Chamber of Commerce. He donated his maps to the Monroe County Historical Society in October 1952 and died six months later, on April 18, 1953.

Today, the only remnants of Port Creek are the road that bears its name, the cemetery and the renovated schoolhouse.

Chapter 4

BEDFORD TOWNSHIP

BULLOCKVILLE

Not much is known about the hamlet of Bullockville other than that it is thought to be named after an early settler of the area. B. Ellis Bullock owned a lot of land, as shown on the 1901 Lang map. There was a one-room wooden schoolhouse named Bullock School built in 1892 on Secor and Anthony Roads; the school was actually on Bullock's property. The school went up to eighth grade, and all the pupils were taught in one classroom. Madeline Johnson Elliot Reger taught sixty pupils there during World War I and said it was regarded as "not an easy school to handle although the parents were most cooperative." She was paid the sum of sixty dollars a month. Many of the students had brothers serving in the war, and she knit a pair of stockings for each of them. On February 23, 1945, the school was completely consumed by fire; it is thought that the fire started because of an overheated furnace.

Incidentally, a drain was dug sometime before 1901 that shows up on the 1901 Lang map as the "Bullock drain," located by Anthony Road.

FORTUNA

Fortuna was a settlement in 1918 located near the Ohio border. There is a Fortuna Road between Smith and West Sterns Roads; otherwise, little else

DT&I train wreck at Fortuna. *Monroe County Library System, Bedford.*

is known about the settlement. But one thing that Fortuna is known for is a train wreck on the Detroit, Toledo and Ironton Railroad. Unfortunately, the wreck left the engineer scalded by hot steam, and he did not survive. Fortuna was mentioned in the *Monroe Evening News* from 1921 through 1923.

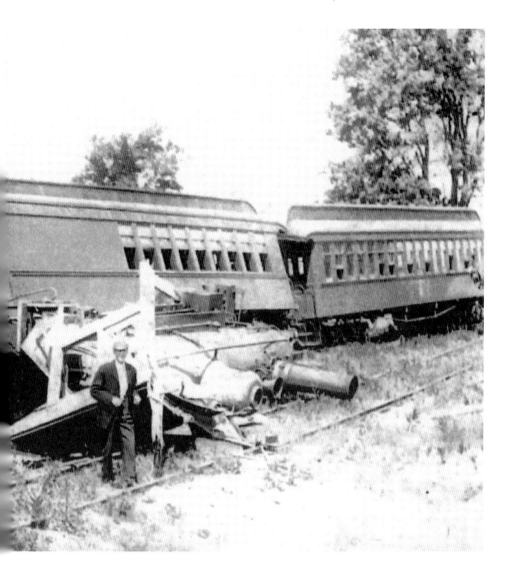

LIBERTY CORNERS

Liberty Corners was never actually a settlement but grew out of four families: Bibb, Hoffman, Lowe and May. Each family owned property in Liberty Corners. The first building erected was the Liberty Corners one-room schoolhouse, built at the junction of Jackman and Sterns Roads before 1859. In 1869, a new brick school was constructed diagonally just across the road on the southeast corner. It sustained damage from a storm

Former Liberty Corners School, built 1869. *Author.*

Former Liberty Corners Church, built 1880. *Author.*

in 1920 but was repaired. It was enlarged in 1925 and was once again damaged, this time by a tornado, in 1948 but was fixed and ran until 1979. It was sold in 1987.

In 1880, Pastor J.B. Sellick built a Wesleyan church on land donated by the Bibb family. The school and church were believed to be all that was ever erected in Liberty Corners—until a grisly discovery was made. When a playground was being put in at the school, tombstones and bones were discovered.

Today, the schoolhouse is now a restaurant, part of a shopping mall at 1675 Sterns Road, and the church is privately owned. There are markers at the church, the shopping mall and the intersection of West Sterns and Jackman Road. Liberty Corners appears on a 1972 map of Lambertville.

LITTLE LAKE

Little Lake is actually a small lake in the northern part of Bedford Township. But throughout its history, it has been known to be as dry as a bone and, at other times, a very large sinkhole. The community of Little Lake was probably named after this body of water. In 1878, it was a station on the Ann Arbor Railroad, at Erie Road. It received a post office on August 11, 1873, which ran until December 30, 1879, with William S. Tuttle as the first postmaster. The post office appears in the 1876 Beers atlas.

The community had a log schoolhouse called the Little Lake School as well, on Erie Road (in the Beers atlas, "S.H." denotes a schoolhouse). The Tuttle children attended this school, and it appears to have been open until 1868. Across from the school was the First Free Will of Little Lake Baptist Church of Bedford and Erie, on Erie Road. In 1892, the church was sold in order to build a new one. Edmond Dull bought it for $101, moved it closer to Temperance and utilized it as a storage facility.

Edmond Dull was born on February 1, 1863, in Pennsylvania to Joseph C. and Mary Benton Dull. He moved with his family to Bedford in 1865. He was a carpenter and a merchant and married Caroline Anstead in 1884 at the Little Lake Baptist Church. They had four children. In 1889, he was highway commissioner for Bedford Township. He also served as township treasurer in 1890, 1891, 1900 and 1901. On November 4, 1902, he was elected to the Monroe County Sherriff's Office, where he served eight years until his tragic death in 1910.

On August 1, 1910, while in the line of duty, Sheriff Dull was hot on the trial of a suspect who had robbed a man and thrown him off a train. Dull chased him south of Erie to the Rau farm. Dull was able to record the incident:

> *I ordered him to throw up his hands* [and his] *reply was to pull a revolver and fire before I could draw my gun. I fell at first shot, which struck me in the right wrist and broke it. I supported myself as best I could in my wounded arm and pulled my gun with my left hand. He shot me twice more and I felt the pain in my left side and stomach, but I sent four bullets after him.*

Dull was rushed to Robinwood Hospital in Toledo, Ohio, where he ultimately succumbed to his wounds on August 3, at age forty-seven. Two separate funeral services were held for the popular sheriff on August 5. The *Monroe Record Commercial* wrote: "Thus has passed away among us a man whom any community could ill spare. He was absolutely fearless and it was this element which in the end, brought about his tragic death."

A suspect, William Harris, was arrested for the crime and—coincidentally, on the day of the funeral—confessed his guilt. He was transferred to Detroit for his own safety and then returned to Monroe on August 16 for his trial. He immediately pled guilty and within a half hour was on a train again, this time bound for the Marquette state prison, sentenced to life in solitary confinement and hard labor. Later, it was discovered that Harris had also been on the lam for a murder in Ontario, Canada.

SAMARIA

Samaria was originally called Weeksville after Elijah Weeks, who was born in New York in 1826 and moved to Bedford Township in the 1840s. He opened a store in the community, married and had a family of eight children. Weeksville's name was changed to Samaria after Elijah's son Sam, who was the first postmaster in 1879. He was also a storekeeper and the township's treasurer. He died at twenty-eight years of age on February 10, 1882, in his home of inflammation of the bowels.

There was a rough oak corduroy road in Samaria that had one toll booth on the west side of the road, just past Erie; the other was about five miles south of it. The village grew up in 1872 between Lewis and Jackman Roads, alongside the railroad station for the Toledo, Ann Arbor and

Top: Elijah Weeks home, Samaria. *Monroe County Library System, Bedford.*

Bottom: Former Elijah Weeks home today. *Author.*

Grand Trunk Railroad. The post office opened in 1879, and the mail was delivered to the Ann Arbor Railroad depot. Samaria still has a post office today that was originally Tracy's Store. Eventually, Samaria had a number of railroad offices, an express office, a telegraph office, two sawmills, a blacksmith shop, a wagon shop, a barrel-making shop, three stores and a cheese factory on Porter Street that ran from 1892 to 1899. John Yager of

Left: Tracy's Store, Samaria. *Monroe County Library System, Bedford.*

Below: Former Tracy's Store today. *Author.*

Top: Cheese factory, Samaria. *Monroe County Library System, Bedford.*

Bottom: Former Cheese factory today. *Author.*

Ida opened a meat market in 1885, and a Mr. Harnden produced hoops for coopers to use.

Roger Willard, who was born in Ida in 1839, moved to the settlement in 1863 and served as postmaster for eight years and as justice of the peace; he also operated a general store. Joseph C. Dull, father of Edmond Dull (refer to the "Little Lake" section), was born in Pennsylvania in 1825 and moved to Samaria in 1869. He worked as a farmer and a carpenter and served as highway commissioner for six terms, as well as holding several township offices.

Theophilus Osgood came from New York to the area and built the First Baptist Church and his own house from stone he and his son carried from Stoney Ridge. He ran a limestone kiln near Stoney Ridge, which he used to make plaster and cement for his house and other buildings. He created a picket fence machine with which he made picket rails. But he did not stop there; he also ran a sorghum and cider mill and made brooms out of corn. It was also believed that Osgood used his farm as a station on the Underground Railroad where he hid slaves escaping from the South on their way to freedom in Canada. He also conducted them to the next safe stop.

Another Samaria-area resident involved in the Underground Railroad was Hall Deland, the "Nighthawk." When slaves came through from Sylvania, Ohio, Deland took them to the French settlers along the Detroit River, who ferried them across to Canada. Sometimes they were taken to Toledo or to Detroit Avenue by Lake Erie, through Monroe and then on

Former Hall "Nighthawk" Deland home today. *Author.*

up to Canada. Hall Deland was sympathetic to the cause and hid the slaves in his large cellar, which had three basements, with the two lowest used to conceal the slaves. From his house, he would take the fugitives by covered wagon through the night to an unknown place closer to Canada.

Deland was born on August 9, 1796, in Massachusetts. He married Laura Goodrich in 1816 at Vernon, Oneida County, New York, and they had three children, Rudolph, Charles and Henry. It appears he came to Monroe in 1850, according to his War of 1812 pension records. He lived at the corner of Samaria and Summerfield Roads. He ran a tavern called the Half-way House; in later years, it was called the Packard House. He died in 1878 and is buried at the Lambertville Methodist Cemetery, but his gravestone does not mention anything about his role in the Underground Railroad.

The one-room Samaria School was built at the junction of Samaria and Jackman Roads in 1869 and, in the 1890s, was torn down for a new two-story frame school. In 1920, however, the new school succumbed to a tornado and was rebuilt out of the same bricks on Samaria Road; it was closed in 1969. The building can still be seen but has been repurposed.

Next to the school, on Jackman Road, was a burial ground, which apparently started as the Porter family plot for those who died of smallpox. Local historian Don Adams believed there were seven burials there, but on further investigation in 2002, that number was raised to a possible forty. Today, the area is on private property, as so many are. Adams believes there could be as many as twenty more unknown burial grounds in Bedford Township.

At present, Samaria still exists but as an unincorporated community. It can be seen on maps from 1896 up through today, but all that remains of its past are some houses and a few renovated buildings.

Smith's Siding

Not much is recorded about Smith's Siding. We know it was a railroad siding, which served as a separate track for a train to pull off to the side. It was located at the intersection of Sylvania, Metamora and Mitchaw Roads in what was Monroe County before it was lost in the 1836 Toledo War. Today, that area is in Lucas County. Smith's Siding was mentioned in the *Monroe Evening News* in 1922.

State Line

State Line was actually what it sounds like: an area located on the state line of Michigan and Ohio. It was a station on the Detroit, Monroe and Toledo Railroad in 1864. The State Line Christian School, at 6320 Lewis Avenue, was also located there and still is. Founded in 1873, it was run by the Lewis Avenue Baptist Church and eventually taught students up to the twelfth grade. There was a State Line Cemetery as well.

Antoine Leonard ran the State Line Brickyard from 1865 to 1880. The brick was handmade and called slap brick; it was used to build most of the brick houses in the area. Leonard employed twelve men and made 300,000–500,000 bricks per year. The Erie Presbyterian Church was rebuilt using bricks from this brickyard in 1888.

Antoine's wife and daughter ran the tollhouse, and the family lived there. They collected the toll for use of the narrow Plank Road. The round-trip toll was fifty cents for a double rig and thirty-five cents for a single one. But if you had a blue ticket, you could pass through for free. The road ran for seven miles and ultimately had three tollhouses: one at the beginning, one in the middle and one at the end by the state line. "Gypsies" would come through the area and caused a lot of trouble, according to the Leonard family, although some had fine wagons and many horses. There were also many Native Americans living and moving in the area as well, but they never caused any trouble.

Maxim Benore and John Suller (Sulier) also owned a brickyard on the banks of the Indian Creek on Dean Road, and Obed Smith owned a sawmill there, too. Many large dairy farms were located throughout the vicinity as well.

Today, there still is a road bearing the same name: State Line Road. The 1901 Lang map shows the owners of the brickyard parcels.

Willits (Willets)

By Crabb and East Sterns Road once existed the community of Willits. The settlement grew up alongside the Toledo and Ann Arbor Railroad station at Sterns Road. It got its post office on November 8, 1880, which ran until September 23, 1887, with Harriet M. Lord as the first postmaster.

The community was named after Edwin Willits, who was born on April 24, 1830, in Otto, New York. His family moved to Monroe County when

Former Banner Oak School, built 1871, Willits. *Author.*

he was six years old. Willits had quite the illustrious career. He graduated from the University of Michigan in 1855 and was editor of the *Monroe Commercial* newspaper for six years. From 1860 to 1872, he served on the Michigan State Board of Education. Also, from 1860 to 1862, he was the chief prosecuting attorney of Monroe County. He was the United States postmaster of Monroe from 1863 to 1866, appointed by President Lincoln. He served as a member of congress from Michigan's Second Congressional District from 1876 to 1883. He was also the first assistant U.S. secretary of agriculture and, in 1885, served as president of the State Agricultural College (SAC)— what today is Michigan State University.

Willits was respected and well liked among his peers and students. His secretary at SAC, H.B. Cannon, said:

> *The student body almost at once recognized him as a master hand in administration. There was an atmosphere of hope about him. The students were proud of their president. The venerable look of the man, his fatherly ways, his eagle's eye—all impressed and moved us....He never slept without fearing that something might go wrong and many a night when we were sound asleep he was pacing the campus, keeping watch and ward.*

He died on October 22, 1896, and is buried in Woodland Cemetery in Monroe.

Lord School was built in 1840 (some say 1853) at the corner of Sterns and Crabb Roads. It was so named after the Lord family farm across the road. In 1871, a new, larger building was constructed, and in 1927, its name was changed to Banner Oak. It was used until 1955 and was Monroe's first high school. Later, it was used for various purposes, and in 1978, it was decided to restore the old school. Today, it is on the Michigan State Register of Historic Sites.

The historical marker on the site says: "A tall oak grew in the yard of Lord School built on the NE corner of Sterns & Crabb Roads in 1853. Julius Sterns unfurled a United States banner from the tree in 1863 to prove his patriotism and hatred of slavery."

Today, nothing exists of Willits but the schoolhouse.

Chapter 5

BERLIN TOWNSHIP

ALEXANDRIA

Alexandria was an early settlement drawn out in 1837 in the Monroe County deed books. It was eventually overtaken by Newport.

BERLIN VILLAGE/HURON STATION (ROCKWOOD)

Berlin Village was drawn up in 1871 in the Monroe County deed books. It was in section 16 of Berlin Township, and the 1876 Beers atlas renames it Rockwood and shows a close-up map of it. But later the area became known as South Rockwood, with Rockwood being located further north. Berlin Village had a stave mill, a store, a brickyard, a wagon shop, a blacksmith shop, a saloon and a school.

South Rockwood Village School shows up on the 1859 Geil map and was located at Brandon and Egypt Roads. In the 1870s, the one-room wooden school was replaced with a larger brick school. A new two-story school was built in front of the old one in 1925 and was utilized until 1958. The school was torn down a few years later. Today, the tunnel that ran under the railroad tracks for the students is the only remnant that still exists.

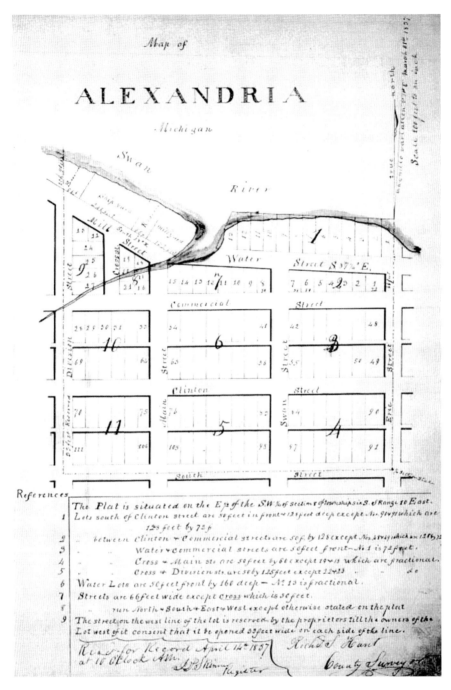

Above: Map of Alexandria, Berlin Township, 1837. *Monroe County Deeds.*

Opposite: Map of Berlin Village, 1871. *Monroe County, Deeds.*

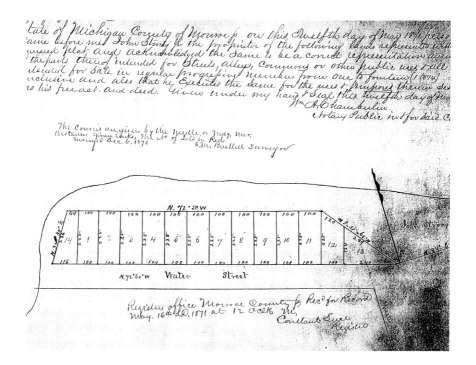

CHAPMAN

Chapman was basically a controlled siding for the CN Shoreline Railroad. North and South Chapman were located in South Rockwood. South Chapman was by North Dixie Highway, while North Chapman was by Huron River Drive. Eventually, the hamlet had a school and a town hall. Its name came from all the Chapmans who lived in the area.

The Chapman School was built by Austin Bostwick Chapman, on North Dixie Highway, south of Sigler Road, in the early 1850s. Austin hired Sarah Cook to be the first schoolteacher. She lived with the family for one dollar a week while teaching. The school lasted until 1905, when Hiram and Martha Chapman donated some land for a larger wood-frame school that was built just north of the original school. It was used until 1947, when it merged with Airport Schools. Hiram was Austin's son. Austin and his wife had three children.

Austin Chapman also built his own Victorian-style home in 1876 for $8,000 and made his own brick to form the three-layer walls that contained an air space between them. The home still looks original and stands at 10995 North Dixie Highway.

Former Austin Bostwick Chapman House, Berlin. *Author.*

Chapman shows up on the 1859 Geil map, the 1901 Lang map and a 1930 map.

GREENVILLE

Greenville was a little hamlet that existed on Swan Creek Road, just east of Dixie Highway. There is still a Greenville Road in the area, but that is about it.

NEWPORT CENTRE

Newport Centre was an area between the railroad tracks off Swan Creek and Brandon Roads. Francisco Brothers Stave Mill was located there. By 1901, Newport Centre had disappeared from most maps. It was taken over by Newport Station, which was located right next to it to the west.

Newport Station (Newport Today)

In December 1855, Newport Station developed into a boomtown spurred on by the Lakeshore, Michigan and Southern Railroad (LS&M) station at Swan Creek and Brandon Roads. Over a twenty-five-year span, the village boasted a gristmill, a cannery, a basket factory, a creamery, a cheese factory, hoop-and-stave mills, a general store, hardware stores, two hotels, a school, and many saloons. Also, a quarry was established at Brandon Road in the late 1800s.

The Herman F. Niedermeier family made an indelible mark on the development of the area. Herman was born in 1804 in Germany, and in 1852, he made his home in Newport. Herman's oldest son, by his first wife, Anna Elizabeth Richtsmeier, was Frederich Christopher Niedermeier. He was instrumental in the founding of Berlin Township and the Newport area. After Frederich became a widower, he met his soon-to-be second wife, Julia Knapp, in 1866, and they married. They made their home on four hundred acres on Dixie Highway. The newlyweds ended up having eight children.

Berlin Township did not exist yet; the whole area was part of Ash Township. But Frederich and some other landowners drafted a petition in November 1867 suggesting that another township be carved out of the eastern area of the large Ash Township. They were successful in their quest and met to elect a supervisor and name the new township. Frederich found himself elected as supervisor; he protested, saying he was not even born there. They asked him where he was born, and he answered Berlin, Germany—and thus the township's name was born.

Frederich had a very successful political career, holding the offices of not only supervisor but also clerk and treasurer for many years. He also served as treasurer of Monroe County from 1875 to 1880.

Frederich's son Julius A. Niedermeier opened a general store and meat market. His store was the only one to have an icehouse for selling fresh meat. Stores carried a lot of smoked meat back then because ice could be hard to come by, and many families had their own icehouse filled with ice packed in sawdust. Unfortunately, Julius passed away at only forty-four years of age, but his wife, Ida, and son Bernard took over the store until it perished in the infamous February 13, 1923 fire that destroyed half the town.

Frederich's brother, Herman F. Jr., married Louisa Kittenger. After farming a while, Herman bought the Gambee Store in Newport and reopened it in October 1900. Five years later, the family moved the Gambee Store further back and built a new store out of concrete block in front of it on Swan Creek

Top: Niedermeier & Sons Store, circa 1905, Newport. *Monroe Publishing Company.*

Bottom: Former Niedermeier & Sons Store today. *Author.*

Top: LS&M Railroad Depot, 1855, Newport. *Monroe Publishing Company.*

Bottom: Newport Church (former LS&M Railroad Depot) today. *Author.*

Road, called H. Niedermeier & Sons. It opened in October 1905. Today, what was once the large store is the home of the Swan Creek Apartments.

In 1887, the Buhl family donated land for a church, and the Methodist-Congregational Church was born. Later, in 1945, it became the Newport Community Church, located at 8823 Swan Creek Road.

Sometime before 1859, the Newport School was built on Newport Road. In 1872, a two-room schoolhouse was built in the same location next to the Methodist church but was destroyed by a tornado in 1918. It was rebuilt at the same site in 1919. It was consolidated into the Newport School District in 1972, and the Newport Community Church purchased it. In 1945, the church also purchased the LS&M Railroad depot and moved it to the site.

P.F. Dusing ran a saloon, as did Robert Navarre, but with a store attached to his. John F. Colburn built a two-story brick general store sometime before 1860. It eventually became LaDuke's Saloon and other businesses over time before it was torn down. Next to Colburn's was Leo Martin's saloon by the railroad tracks on Swan Creek Road. Bernard Niedermeier later opened a grocery store in Martin's saloon. Martin had to close because of Prohibition.

Around 1890, Anthony Neckel & Son built a gristmill/hardware store at what is now 8700 Swan Creek Road; Neckel produced buckwheat flour and marketed it successfully as pancake flour. On February 13, 1913, a huge fire

Martin's Place saloon, Newport. *Monroe Publishing Company.*

Anthony Neckel & Son store, circa 1890, Newport. *Monroe Publishing Company.*

on the north side of Swan Creek destroyed all the buildings and businesses, including the mill. The mill was rebuilt by the Partlen brothers and operated for another twenty-five years.

There was also a blacksmith and woodworking shop run by Adolphus Minor; Newport House Hotel, run by Mary Valade; and the Newport Bank, established by Dr. Jerome J. Valade.

The Brandon Road Stone Quarry at the corner of Swan Creek and Brandon Roads, on the J. Labeau property, is shown in the 1876 Beers atlas as "SQ," meaning "stone quarry." In the 1880s, during an excavation, gold specks were found in the rock, and everyone was suddenly hit with gold fever—the rumor of gold spread like wildfire. When samples were analyzed, however, it was found not to be real gold, and everyone was devastated.

In 1903, the quarry was a Detroit United Railways operation for obtaining crushed stone for the roadbed of a double track railway. The quarry was about two acres on the surface and ninety feet deep. Shortly after this, it was allowed to fill in, was sold and became privately owned. In the 1960s, it was a popular swimming spot. Today, it is fenced off with no access.

Newport Station had absorbed Newport Centre on most maps by 1901. By 1911, however Newport Station had started to disappear off maps itself and instead became Newport, which it still is today, located at Swan Creek and Brandon Roads.

Even though Newport Station is Newport today, much has changed from its industrious past. Many buildings no longer exist, and some that do have been repurposed, but there are still some original homes in the area.

OLD PORT

Old Port (which was Newport at the time) was founded by William Tandy White. William was the son of Enoch White and Betsy Tandy; he was born on March 26, 1807, in Newport, New Hampshire. He came to Monroe in 1831 and established the town of Newport, naming it after his hometown, in 1835. The post office was established in 1837 with White as postmaster; however, the National Archives says it was established in 1836 with Sanford Hopkins as the first postmaster. In any case, it was located at the intersection of Swan Creek Road and North Dixie Highway. Incidentally, Newport was originally called "Riviere Aux Signes." White was a farmer by trade and also established a sawmill, a general store, a nursery, a greenhouse and the Stage and Steamboat Hotel. He served for thirty years as postmaster, and he was also a justice of the peace.

White married Nancy Reynolds on February 16, 1837, and they had eleven children. He died on November 22, 1866, in Newport at age fifty-nine. Although various individuals owed him $20,000, he canceled their debts because he knew they were too poor to pay him. He left an estate worth over $100,000.

According to Newport author T. Victor Menard:

> The original settlement thrived and grew for almost twenty years at which point in the mid-1850s the new railroads drew business a mile and a half to the west. Soon the original settlement became a lost town. White's Newport became known as Old Newport, and eventually Oldport. Of the prominent diehards remaining in the area were Charlie Cousino and Peter Beaubien. Both operated saloons within the steeple of St. Charles Church. The Beaubien complex at Dixie Highway and Swan Creek Roads (now the location of the public access site) included a saloon, hardware store and family residence.

The first railroad that changed everything came in 1856: the Detroit, Monroe & Toledo Railroad (DM&T) at Swan Creek Road and North Dixie Highway. Later, this became the Michigan Southern & Northern Indiana

Railroad. The DM&T put in a depot in the Newport Station area that would run until the 1930s.

In 1873, the Toledo, Canada Southern and Detroit Railway (originally the Chicago & Canada Southern Railroad) built a line to tap into the Toledo and Detroit markets. The line was laid east of and parallel to the first railroad. It was actually closer to Old Port but instead helped to develop the area northwesterly between the lines that would become known as Newport Centre, at the crossroads of Swan Creek Road and Drew Street. This area, with Newport Station and Swan Creek and Brandon Roads right next to it, continued to boom, while Old Port started to decline. Incidentally, this was part of the reason for the downfall of Brest in Frenchtown Township as well, according to Menard.

On old maps, such as the 1876 Beers atlas and the 1901 Lang map, the name Newport is still used. It was not until the mid-1900s that Old Port started showing up more on maps and the name Newport was moved to where Newport Station and Newport Centre were once located.

The Old Port School was built in 1859 on Bomiea Road. By 1876, a second school had been built on North Dixie Highway; it was renamed Bomia (Bomya) in 1932 and then became part of Jefferson Schools in 1948.

In 1852, land was donated for a church, and in 1853, the wooden St. Charles Borromeo Catholic Church was born. The same year, land was donated for the cemetery. In 1882, the Masserant family donated land for the present brick parish, which was completed in 1886. There are two cemeteries, the old one from 1853 and the current one.

Prohibition completely enveloped the area simply because of its proximity to the water and to Canada. Berlin Township is described on a 2020 historical marker as "A Bootleggers' Paradise: Residents and out-of-town professionals alike were caught moving booze through Berlin Township. Violence and death became commonplace during the Prohibition years. Bootleggers' bodies were found bullet-ridden, washed up on the shore or left in abandoned shacks. Others drowned, falling through the winter ice."

The area's proximity to Lake Erie also brought gangsters on their way to Canada on the run after a crime spree, such as John Dillinger, in 1934. Dillinger was rumored to be in the area of Horseshoe Bend by Estral Beach. Dillinger, a notorious bank robber accused of robbing twenty-four banks and also shooting a policeman, was supposedly hiding out in one of the beach cottages. He had escaped from an Indiana prison by threatening guards with a wooden pistol. Ohio deputies received a tip that Dillinger

St. Charles Borromeo Catholic Church, Oldport. *Author.*

was in the vicinity; they joined Monroe County officers in the search but were not able to locate the criminal.

An unfortunate incident etched into the memory of many Newport residents occurred in May 1905. It was called the worst wreck in the history of the Detroit, Monroe & Toledo Shoreline. On Friday, May 5, 1905, the

Monroe Democrat reported that the accident occurred the previous Saturday night at the curve just north of Newport. Two trains crashed headlong into each other at a high rate of speed, leaving two people dead and another twenty injured, some seriously. The northbound car was supposed to wait on the sidetrack until the southbound car passed, unless other orders were received. No orders came through, and the train neglected to exit onto the sidetrack and wait but instead continued on the main track. Suddenly, the southbound train came whirling around the curve at a high rate of speed. The next sound was that of crashing metal, wood and iron. The scene was a horrific one, with the cars heaped on top of each other in a mangled, crumpled-up mess.

The investigation into what happened revealed that multiple issues contributed to the accident. One issue was the new, confusing schedule of how and when to get orders—and in this case, the orders were not received at all. Furthermore, Conductor Bale of the northbound train was also delayed trying to remove a belligerent, intoxicated passenger from the train. He was distracted, and once the train got going again, he forgot to get off at the sidetrack. If this unfortunate incident had not occurred, the trains might have had time to see each other before the curve where they met.

Today, the St. Charles Church complex and cemetery still dominate Oldport. Some older homes and a few buildings remain, but not much else.

Petersburgh

Petersburgh was named after the Peters family, who owned a lot of property in the area; as shown on the 1859 Geil map. The name Petersburgh appears in the 1876 Beers atlas under the business section, and there were many businesses in the area. The location was just northwest of Rockwood in the northern part of Berlin Township. There was the Zibbell House Hotel, three general stores, a meat market, a blacksmith, two wagon shops, a cabinetmaking shop, a sawmill, a shingle mill, a gristmill, a stave mill, a cheese factory and a saloon.

A meat market or butcher shop could prove quite handy for the homemaker. Whenever there were trimmings left over from butchering, homemade lye soap could be made. To make lye soap, a barrel was filled to the brim with wood ash. Then a hollow area was made by pressing down the ash, into which water was poured. The water drained through holes in the barrel onto a board that let it flow into a crock. It started out brown in color and gradually grew lighter as it came out. Then it was boiled with the rinds, tallow and trimmings left over from butchering. Once it reached the right thickness, it was allowed to cool and then cut into bars.

In the 1876 Beers atlas, a Presbyterian church and the Peters School show up. The school was located at the intersection of Armstrong and Dauncy Roads. After 1901, the school was rebuilt just south of the original school site at 13623 Armstrong Road; it closed in 1946. It is a private residence today.

Today, the Petersburgh area is part of the greater Rockwood and Flat Rock vicinity.

Chapter 6

DUNDEE TOWNSHIP

(VAN NESS' MILLS)

BRAGG

Bragg was founded by Ebenezer Bragg, originally from New York, who settled in the heavily wooded area in 1840. He donated some of his farmland for the Bragg School. The former Bragg School is located at 19979 Bragg and Cake Roads and is a private residence today. It was built around 1880 and was used until 1943. There is also the Leib Cemetery in the middle of a field off the north side of Cake Road. There is a boulder with a bronze plaque on it that states that the cemetery was donated in 1862 by Civil War veteran Michael Leib and his wife, Caroline.

DIANN

Although listed in some places as a settlement, Diann was actually an interlocked railroad crossing of the Detroit, Toledo and Ironton (DT&I) and Ann Arbor main lines. It was located about three miles south of Dundee. Henry Ford owned the DT&I Railroad and created the crossing at Diann. Ford built a connection for both rail lines with a block signal as well as a robust mechanical interlocking tower run by electricity.

Henry Ford purchased the DT&I Railroad in 1920; at the time, it was called the "railroad to nowhere." The railroad had gone bankrupt multiple times. It was in horrendous shape, but Ford paid $5 million to acquire it. He knew the potential it could offer him: shipping from his plants at Highland Park and the Rouge all the way down to Ironton, Ohio, especially since it crossed every New York-Chicago trunk line. The mainline ran a distance of 378 miles. Spending $15 million overall, Ford wasted no time reorganizing the company and rebuilding the tracks, bridges and maintenance buildings; before long, he had the railroad beyond respectable again. He also built employee morale and offered higher wages than other railroad companies. The railroad was turning a profit again and gaining a good reputation.

With that accomplished, Ford could turn his attention to one of the things he did best: experimenting. Electric railways were nothing new in cities, but they were primarily used for passenger transport. Ford wanted an electric railway for commercial interests. Around 1926, he electrified the railway route for about forty miles from the River Rouge to Flat Rock and planned to continue the route westerly through Monroe County, passing through Carleton and on to Maybee. A series of catenaries (arches) for the electric lines had to be built about every two hundred to three hundred feet to accomplish this. Many are still visible in the Dearborn area. Although the concrete foundations can be seen all the way to Maybee, the catenaries were

DT&I catenaries (arches). *Author.*

never built that far. Ford also built two giant heavy-duty electric engines, meant to operate as a pair, just for this purpose.

In 1929, Ford sold the railroad to the Pennsylvania Railroad for a hefty profit. He had grown tired of federal regulations governing the railroads and decided to concentrate on his automobiles again.

Today, Diann is inaccessible, and nothing remains of it except the railroad track going through on Gloff Road.

DURBAN

Durban was a location on the DT&I line that developed as a result of Henry Ford building a straight line for the DT&I Railroad from Diann to Malinta, Ohio. It was named after F.A. Durban, who was president of the DT&I and the Ann Arbor Railroads before Ford came in. It was located west of Maybee in the area of Stewart and Sheets Roads.

But Durban became best known for what happened on October 20, 1922. That night, around midnight, people were awakened for miles around by a loud thundering, screeching noise. It turned out that two heavy freight trains with the new "Ford engines" had come into Durban—one, going west, right after the other, going east. But suddenly, the tracks malfunctioned and spread apart as one of the trains went over it, leaving the huge engine and sixteen cars to fall between the two tracks and into a ditch. Four of the cars landed on top of each other, causing a mangled, twisted-up mess. One of the cars was hauling a load of young cattle, but amazingly, they all escaped with their lives; only one was injured. Unfortunately, the engineer and the fireman were severely scalded by the hot steam, and the brakeman was also severely injured. They were taken to Maybee right away to be treated by Dr. Kaumeyer. The engine had burrowed so deeply into the ground that it took two wrecking cranes to lift it out.

EGYPT/MILWAUKEE

The community of Egypt, also called Milwaukee, was located about four miles west and one and a half miles north of Dundee in an area known as Bear Swamp. It was bounded by Milwaukee Road to the south, Cone Road to the north, Petersburg Road to the east and Dennison Road to the west.

Egypt got its name from Joseph and Mary Green, a poor couple living there. Joe had to have his coat patched so many times to make it last that it looked like Joseph's biblical coat, according to one story passed down. Apparently, he was on his way to Rea in a wagon when someone saw him and remarked, "Here comes Joseph with his coat of many colors down out of the land of Egypt." The name held on for over seventy-five years.

Egypt was considered a backward, unsavory place, with families that lived there in little more than shacks. It was the perfect hideout for criminals and gangsters, especially during Prohibition. The area was heavily wooded and supported itself by selling wood. The French settlers used the towering white oak trees to make ship masts, and the trees were logged out for charcoal. Once the area was depleted, farms sprang up.

In 1876, the Crow (or Crowe) School opened on Day and Hiser Roads for children living in the Egypt area. It was named after the farmer Roger S. Crow, whose half acre of land was leased for the school at $1.50 annually; eventually he sold it to the school for $50. He was keen on education and was a school official for twenty-five years. In the early nineteenth century, the school was renamed Egypt. In 1876, there were twenty-four students enrolled; by spring of 1877, nineteen more had enrolled, including three-year-old Emma Keene. Teachers were paid $60 for the year. On July 19, 1890, under the cover of darkness, someone broke into the schoolhouse and set it on fire, destroying it. It was rebuilt in brick at the same spot and ran until 1948; today, it is no longer there.

Sunday school was taught at the school since there was no church in Egypt; the nearest church was in Azalia. People were buried either in the Azalia Cemetery or the cemetery on Dennison Road, called the Rice Cemetery. Milwaukee Road was a corduroy road—built of logs—and was very muddy; sometimes the carriage wheels sank all the way down to the hubs in the mud, making travel all but impossible.

Around the beginning of the nineteenth century, Egypt had many mills. The Bunce brothers owned charcoal mills on Milwaukee Road, and Dan Reeves opened a sawmill in the heart of the swamp. There was a sawmill and a brick and tile mill located between Petersburg and Platt Roads as well. A general store was also located there. There were many charcoal kilns made of brick, with no chimneys and rounded tops. Holes located at the bottom were sealed shut once the fire was started to restrict the intake of oxygen and let the wood smolder, creating charcoal. The charcoal would be left there for a week or so; then when it cooled, it would be loaded and shipped out to places like Toledo and Ann Arbor.

Rice Cemetery, Milan. *Author.*

Newton Squires and his wife, Alice, bought a farmhouse in Bear Swamp on 120 acres. The house was once part of a logging camp that was used by the logging mill workers. All the workers were fed at long tables in a large, open room. Their son Ransom believes that there were as many as twelve cutters and twenty-five men working at the mill in its heyday. He remembers seven or so logging tram cars on the property. The cars would carry the logs to Cone Road, where they would be put on wagons and taken to neighboring towns. Roads were built in the swamp area for the tram cars. Split logs were used to form the bed by laying them crossways. Then steel rails were laid on top, about twelve feet apart. The trams themselves were about fifteen feet long. Horses were used to pull the heavy loaded tram cars; each car had a hand brake in case it careened out of control.

The logging camp had been abandoned for ten to fifteen years before the Squires came along. They had not been there long, however—they'd just barely settled in—when a big flood destroyed all their crops, and they had to leave for a couple years. When they returned, they built a new brick house. Unfortunately, they were hit with another disaster in 1923 when a large fire consumed their home and they lost everything.

Another couple, Byron and Martha Lafler, settled in the heavily forested Bear Swamp along Milwaukee Road. When Byron was thirty-six, he built a log cabin for his sixteen-year-old bride. Through the years, he worked clearing out the land. He also got help from the neighbors when he set up a "logging bee"—basically a land-clearing party complete with food and beer. Gertrude, their daughter (who ended up marrying William Noble), remembers going to school at the Egypt/Milwaukee School, which was located in the middle of the swamp. Gertrude recalls her teacher Etta Cavanaugh, who, in 1897, presented the pupils with a Christmas gift: a card with a photograph of herself and the names of all sixty-five students enrolled there. All the students pooled their money to buy a gift for her: a rocking chair.

On the rare occasion of a school board member passing away, the school would close, and the students would get to view the deceased in the casket at the funeral. Gertrude remembers well when Samuel Williams passed away. She said he was out in the woods alone, blasting out stumps with dynamite, when he got too close. She claimed that she and her classmates were not scared to go to the funeral but were "fascinated" instead.

During these times, many families contended with epidemics, and Gertrude's family was no exception. Typhoid fever went through her family in 1890, and she caught it, but luckily no one perished from it, although her sister was close. Unfortunately for Gertrude, she also caught scarlet fever.

But when Gertrude was eight, a horrible event took place that was forever etched in her mind. She was outside when, suddenly, their house caught fire, along with part of the town. The neighbors pitched in, throwing buckets of water on the flames—but since there was no fire station, there was no way to stop the raging inferno, and all was lost. The sawmill, the general store and other houses also burned. This forced Gertrude's family to relocate, and they moved to Azalia.

Egypt/Milwaukee no longer exists today; farm fields and a few houses dot the landscape, but that is about it. Egypt shows up on a 1941 map under Dundee.

Five Points

Five Points was an area on M-50 about half a mile east of Dundee where five roads intersected. There was a dance hall there that hosted many dances and live music. The venue was often advertised in the local newspaper in the late 1920s.

During Prohibition, resident Joe Zuraski of Five Points was charged with violating the Eighteenth Amendment. He was caught with a forty-gallon still and two hundred gallons of moonshine. Zuraski was sentenced in Monroe and plead guilty.

Today, the Dundee Liquor Store at 5-Points is located at the intersection.

Petersburg Junction

Petersburg Junction was located about a mile northwest of Petersburg, between Lulu and Albain Roads, and bisected by Teal Road. It served as a crossing of the Detroit, Toledo and Ironton (DT&I) Railroad, but in 1931, the operators, levelmen and switch tenders were removed. Even though the crossing was no longer used, the junction continued to be a point of interest. There was even a schoolhouse, Reynolds School, at Petersburg and Brewer Roads, which is now in very poor condition. Petersburg Junction appeared on a 1941 map and a 1972 map of Dundee.

Rea (Millersville, Miller's Crossing, Clarksville)

About six miles west of Dundee was the settlement known as Rea. It was originally known as Millersville or Clarksville, after Clark Miller, the blacksmith. In 1875, Farmer William Rea came to the area and settled on Day Road at the end of what became Rea Road. He became well known because he owned a large threshing machine, so the settlement was renamed after him. On March 2, 1844, Rea received its post office, which operated until October 2, 1906; Charles C. Huggett was the first postmaster. It could not be named Clarksville because one already existed, so the name Rea was adopted for the post office. Then, in 1866, Rea became a station on the Michigan & Ohio Railroad, with E.L. Moore as the station agent. Later, the railroad became the Detroit, Toledo & Milwaukee Railroad.

Rea had a school at the corner of Monk and Kent Roads that was known as Kent School, Moore School and Ray School throughout its history. It was built prior to 1859; it may have been updated at some point, and it ran until 1947. It no longer exists.

In 1873, church services were held in the schoolhouse. It was decided to build a church. The land was donated by Homer Miller, and in 1874, the

Rea today, Dundee. *Author.*

church was finished. It was known as the Rea Methodist Church at Kent and Rea Roads. On April 12, 1893, the church was almost destroyed by a tornado, and much of it had to be rebuilt. The church consolidated with Azalia Church in 1967 and the building closed; it was torn down in 1976. But the bell was saved and is now at the Dundee Old Mill Museum.

There was a small cemetery just north of Rea by the river on Petersburg Road. There used to be some tombstones there, but they disappeared, and eventually someone built a house on the site, as happened to many of these small, obscure cemeteries.

At the beginning of the twentieth century, Rea had a hotel, a grain elevator, a blacksmith shop and two stores. Jake Hiser ran the blacksmith shop. One general store, just west of the railroad depot, was owned by a Mr. Huggett. Frank Overmyer also ran a general store for over fifty years, where he offered everything "from a needle to a threshing machine." At one point, he even had a grain elevator. Frank also loaded up a wagon with goods and sold them to the families in the area five days a week. He used ice to keep the items fresh. Many times, the farmers' wives would sell or trade eggs and butter with Frank. The store was originally Frank's father's. Frank and his brother Lou ran it, but one day, they got into a terrible fight in which they were wielding axes against each other. Lou stormed out and, ultimately, left the town for good. Overmyer sold his store in the late 1940s, and by 1950, it had closed. It was eventually torn down, and a house was built on the location.

DT&I trainwreck, Rea Road, Dundee, 1910. *Monroe Publishing Company.*

Rea had its share of tragedy. On April 12, 1893, most of the town was leveled by a tornado. Blacksmith Jake Hiser's wife, Marian, was killed in the storm. Also, there was a train wreck on Rea Road between Rea and Dundee on March 14, 1910. A Detroit, Toledo and Ironton train was northbound with cargo when it was discovered that cars were missing from the train. The engine went in reverse at high speed, which made the tracks spread apart. The engine suddenly found itself lying on its side across both rails. The engineer and the fireman were both scalded by steam and bruised but otherwise were alright. It took a heavy crane to lift the engine up.

The last passenger train came through Rea on November 2, 1931—and just three years later, in 1934, no more freight trains were passing through Rea either. Thus, the depot closed and was loaded into a farm wagon to go to its new home in Cone. Ironically, it was almost hit by a train on its way. Not long after the depot closed, the rails were torn up.

Today, there is little left of Rea but a few houses along Kent Road. Kent Road was originally a Native American trail. Rea Road did not exist until the early twentieth century, and there was no bridge over Macon Creek. The railroad tracks are long gone as well. Rea appears in the 1896 Ogle atlas, on the 1901 Lang map and up to 1941 on some Dundee maps.

Chapter 7

ERIE TOWNSHIP
(BAY SETTLEMENT)

ALEXIS (DETROIT JUNCTION)

Alexis was a settlement that developed in 1878 at the crossing of two railroad lines heading south from Detroit. Thus, it was also called the Detroit Junction. It appears on a 1911 Rand McNally map and is part of Ohio today.

HAVRE

Havre was Monroe's version of Atlantis. It all started in 1836, when some speculators from New York—Salmon Kinney, Charles Osgood and Dan Miller—envisioned a bustling harbor town on Halfway Creek in Bedford Township (today's Summit Street in Erie). Salmon Kinney was influential in the founding of Vienna as well, which ultimately became Erie. Dan Miller would go on to become mayor of Monroe. The New Yorkers liked the sheltered, strategic location off Lake Erie with its rich soil. They bought the land from the Morin family of Morin Point. Since the investors were not familiar with the area or Lake Erie's waxing and waning moods, they had no idea what they were in for.

The *Monroe Times* reported on November 24, 1836, that Havre had gone from no houses in March to eleven by November. Plus, the Tavern House, now almost complete, would be the largest and best wooden building in the entire county. There were also plans for five sixty-foot covered docks—

the piles were already going in. A warehouse was set to go in soon as well. All this was in preparation for the beginning of the spring shipping season. The investors dreamed of a commercial port town that would rival Detroit and pull business all the way from Buffalo. Surveys were ordered for two highways to go in that would connect Havre to Dundee one way and to Indiana the other.

Havre did indeed become a bustling harbor town when several businesses located there, including stores, taverns, hotels, offices, warehouses, loading docks, multiple houses, a hat shop and a gristmill. Everything was located at the confluence of the Ottawa River and Havre Bay. A post office was put in on June 19, 1837, and was only open for six months, closing on December 15, 1837. Joshua B. Van Deusen was the first postmaster.

Steamships helped realize the New Yorkers' dreams of a harbor town when Havre became the location for winter storage of many such boats. One was the Buffalo steamboat *Mazeppa*. The harbor and bay provided a safe shelter from Lake Erie's tumultuous waters in the winter. Havre Bay is Maumee Bay today.

Plans for a Havre Branch Railroad that would intersect between Toledo and Adrian and put the town in the crosshairs of the Erie and Kalamazoo Railroad seemed destined to make the investors' dreams of a huge commercial town come true. With connections to Adrian, Toledo and other cities, Havre could not fail. The railroad was incorporated and granted a charter by the State of Michigan in 1836:

> *An Act to incorporate the Havre Branch Rail Road Company, Sec. 1. Be in enacted by the Senate and House of Representatives of the State of Michigan, that Salmon Keeney, Henry S. Platt, David Graham, Charles Osgood, George Hall, Elisha Hayden and Joseph Jackson, be, and they are hereby appointed commissioners.…Sec. 2.…Body corporate and politic, by the name of "The Havre Branch Rail Road Company"….Sec. 3.… Double track or singles track from Havre in Monroe County, running westerly until it shall intersect the Maumee Branch railroad of Erie & Kalamazoo railroad at some suitable or convenient point.*

The investors and farmers were anxious to get the project moving. Part of their justification drew from the idea that it was

> *estimated that the portion of Michigan, south of Toledo and Adrian rail road, and of a line drawn due west from Adrian, is equal to 1440 square*

> *miles, and it comprises one of the finest agricultural portions of that state. It is now settling rapidly with an enterprising population, who are anxious for sending their produce to market through a Michigan avenue, and bring in their merchandise to a Michigan port.…To remedy this state of things, it is desired, by our enterprising citizens in that quarter, that the state, if it engages in any works of internal improvement, should aid in the construction of the Have rail road.*

Just as the citizens begged for, the state appropriated some money, $20,000, for helping with the construction of the Havre railroad in the Improvement Bill passed in March 1837.

For up to six months, articles in the newspapers at the time addressed the area of Havre, and it went from reportedly being the best of places to the worst. Finally, reporters with the *Monroe Times* went to investigate the area for themselves:

> *We have heard…so many contradictory reports…that we recently visited the place…and we are free to say that we were somewhat disappointed when we found that Havre was neither under water nor in a marsh—but upon dry land, surrounded, on the Michigan side, by old settled and fertile farms.…The soil is dark and sandy, and the water of the bay…appears to be clear. This bay makes a fine, spacious, and natural harbor.…Two large and substantial wharves are now nearly finished, and the fact that two of our lake steamboats are now lying there in perfect safety…must convince the doubting of the ample depth of the water of the bay. The objection often urged against Havre in consequence of a part of its grounds being low, might with equal justice be made against Chicago and twenty other towns on our western lakes.*

But the railroad never existed as more than ink on paper. Ironically, all the bickering back and forth in the media was actually valid. The railroad was not the only casualty of the arguments, however. Lake Erie settled the matter once and for all.

Havre's dreams sank into oblivion, just like the town was destined to do within only two years. Since the speculators had never seen the area before, they never knew it was usually underwater. Being only a few feet above lake level, much of the land was usually marsh. In the spring, suddenly, out of the blue, the lake level started rising and did not stop until the whole town was surrounded by water and sinking. In just a few days, Halfway Creek looked

Havre today. *Author.*

like a lake itself, and the whole town was overtaken by up to four feet of cold, rough lake water. Isidore Morin, who originally sold some of the real estate to the investors, wrote about the event: "They rowed their pirogues [canoes] right into the tavern and there the barrels were floating all about. Most of the men had all they wanted to drink for nothing."

People scrambled all over trying to salvage something from their houses and businesses as they sprinted toward higher ground. They planned to return as soon as the water receded, but alas, it never did. They finally realized that their only hope was to return to the town in the winter when the water froze. Havre was once again a bustling town—but this time, people were trying not to build homes or businesses but to salvage them. One resident, Bruce Agnew, recalled his grandfather Jared Agnew (or Egnew) talking about an Atlantis-like scenario in which Havre was "drowned out," with only one building left standing—the gristmill at the end of Harrison Street. The other buildings sank into oblivion or were rescued by being pulled across the ice. Sam LaPointe's grocery store was moved to Eric and Ed Drewyor's tavern to the southeast corner of Dixie Highway and Manhattan Street. Bruce's grandfather managed to drag his house across the ice to Dixie Highway, and it might have been the oldest in Erie. It was eventually turned into a Methodist church, then a home again; it no longer exists today.

There are no traces of the settlement of Havre, except for a marina.

LAKEWOOD, LAKESIDE, VENICE

These areas were located on Lake Erie and ultimately combined to form Luna Pier. Luna Pier was able to finally open its own post office in 1929 because the population was large enough. It was later incorporated as a city in 1963.

But in 1905, Lakewood was a resort with fourteen cottages. At the turn of the century, a streetcar was available to shuttle people from Monroe to the Monroe Piers resort or to Lakeside and Toledo Beach. Undoubtedly, that grew the popularity of the area to the point that thousands of people were coming out to enjoy the long pier jutting out into the lake, built in 1923. That is how the area came to be called Luna Pier (the pier later collapsed).

The area was transformed during Prohibition. It was a hot spot on Lake Erie for Toledoans, who met up there to get their hootch and "bathtub" gin from bootleggers for only two dollars.

Chateau Louise at 4320 Luna Pier Road was built as a general store by Paul Dussia in 1898 and moved to Lakeside just after the beginning of the twentieth century. It had not only room for guests but a barn and stalls for the horses, too. In the early 1930s, Louise Gellar bought the store from Dussia and turned it into the original Chateau Louise restaurant.

Postcard of Lake Wood (Luna Pier). *Author.*

Pretty Boy Floyd hideout (Luna Pier). *Author.*

Charles Arthur Floyd was undoubtedly one of the area's most infamous visitors—alias Pretty Boy Floyd. He became America's most wanted when John Dillinger was caught and killed on July 2, 1934, elevating Floyd to the status of public enemy number one in the eyes of the FBI. Floyd, whose choice of weapon was a machine gun, was running rampant across Ohio committing bank robbery after bank robbery. Then he decided to cross the state line into Michigan.

After robbing a bank in Sylvania on February 5, 1930, he made his getaway in a car with Michigan license plates. He was looking for a nondescript place to hide out, and he found it only six miles from the border at 4408 Luna Pier Road (Lakewood Road).

But Floyd was brash and undaunted, and a couple months later, he decided to try his luck in robbing some Toledo banks. But his luck ran out, and he was caught and ultimately sentenced to fifteen years in the Ohio state penitentiary. Yet that was not the end of the story. While being transported by train, he escaped out an open window and was once again on the lam. He had four more years of freedom, if you will, in which to commit many more robberies before he was caught for the last time. He was running around with a hefty $23,000 bounty on his head, whether he was apprehended dead or alive. The end of the rope for Floyd came just three months after Dillinger met his end. On October 22, 1934, Floyd was discovered around East Liverpool, Ohio. He took cover in a cornfield just north of the city but was surrounded. A hail of gunfire ensued, and this time, he would not escape. His last words were, "I'm done for; you've hit me twice."

The Lakewood area shows up on other maps from 1943 up to 1955 under Erie.

MANHATTAN

The canal port of Manhattan was founded in the early 1830s. The Maumee Bank of Manhattan also originated at this time. The Patterson Hotel was built, and a post office opened in 1836. Daniel Chase served as the first postmaster. Thirty-nine-year-old Seneca Allen moved to Monroe in 1827; he opened a dry goods store at Manhattan, primarily for trading with the Native Americans. He also plotted out the villages of Trenton, Flat Rock and Toledo in 1831.

Manhattan was part of the territory that Michigan lost during the Toledo War in 1836; subsequently, it became part of Lucas County, Ohio. On April 24, 1848, the town was dissolved under court order. The bank was closed, and Manhattan ceased to exist, other than as a road name.

PERRY'S GROVE

Perry's Grove was a small settlement named after Warren Perry, who was the first postmaster. The post office ran from May 2, 1834, to May 17, 1838. Many Perrys owned property in the vicinity, according to the 1859 Geil map.

PORT LAWRENCE (DEPOT, TREMAINVILLE)

In 1832, Stephen B. Comstock and William Oliver purchased land to create the harbor town of Port Lawrence. It was named after the vessel *Lawrence*, which fought in the Battle of Lake Erie during the War of 1812. The town received a post office in 1823, with Benjamin F. Stickney as the first postmaster. In 1834, its name was changed to Tremainville after the brothers

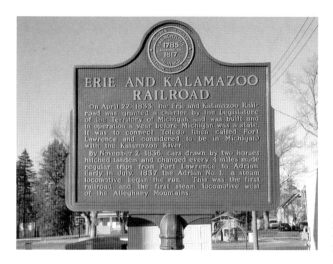

Erie and Kalamazoo Railroad historical marker. *Author.*

Isaac and Calvin Tremain, from New York. But the next day, the post office was changed back to Port Lawrence, with Stephen B. Comstock as postmaster. After the Toledo War in 1836, it became part of Lucas County, Ohio, and is part of Toledo today.

In 1823, the Erie and Kalamazoo Railroad was granted the right to run a line from this area to Kalamazoo. It would not be until 1836, however, that the first section was finished. It was the first horse-powered railroad west of the Alleghenies and the first in Michigan, running between Adrian and Port Lawrence.

VIENNA

Vienna was plotted in 1836 by Christian Hertzler, but by an act of the legislature, its name was changed to Erie in 1850. It was a station in 1858 for the Lakeshore Railroad and, later, the Michigan Central Railroad, which was established in 1882. According to one 1883 account: "The people of Vienna feel very grateful toward General Superintendent Brown of the Michigan Central, for permitting the train which passes that station without stopping to stop and permit a passenger to alight who was summoned home on account of sickness."

One of the first residents, Salmon Keeney from New York, came to the area in 1827. He was originally going to settle in Deerfield, but due to rampant typhoid at the time, he settled in what would become Vienna. It was an unforgettable trip for him and his family. They boarded a schooner at

Buffalo full of hopes for what was to be their new home in Monroe County. Unfortunately, the voyage was plagued by storms and rough water, so much so that the family ran out of provisions and were reduced to one ham, which they gnawed down to the bone. At their stop in Cleveland, they were able to procure more supplies. But as luck would have it, the little boat had a hard time trying to get the supplies to the schooner and ended up losing all its cargo in the cold lake water. The captain, in a hurry to make up time, decided the voyage must go on. When the family finally reached LaPlaisance Bay in Monroe, they were starving and emaciated.

Salmon went on to buy 120 acres by Dixie Highway and with his son, Andrew Jackson, cleared away the heavy timber. He planted the first apple trees in the area, and his legacy survives today in the form of the Keeney-Miller apple orchards in Erie.

Salmon also organized the first English school in the settlement and taught there. Originally known as Turner School after landowner Jacob Turner, it was renamed Keeney after Salmon Keeney. Built of logs in 1833, it was utilized as a church and courthouse too. The school was at the corner of Luna Pier Road (Lakeside Road) and South Dixie Highway. It housed forty

Former Salmon Keeney House today. *Author.*

Former Erie Village School, built 1905. *Author.*

pupils up to the eighth grade. It was later rebuilt with wood in 1834, and Keeney changed its name to Erie School in 1836. In 1861, a new school was constructed of bricks about one hundred yards from the original site; it closed in 1953.

Another school, the Erie Village School, was built around 1850 in Vienna at the junction of Erie and Manhattan Streets. A larger brick school was built after the first one burned down on April 2, 1905. It was recorded that an intoxicated teacher, Leon E. Schafer, set the school on fire and watched it burn from the nearby Presbyterian church. Schafer fled the area but was caught about thirty days later. He confessed and was sentenced to five years in prison. The story goes that after he was released from Jackson Prison, he was rehired as a teacher in Erie; nothing has been found to corroborate that. The present school was shut down in 1951, and today, it is an apartment complex located at 2023 Erie Road.

In 1826, a post office was put in and named Bay Settlement, with Benoni Newkirk as the first postmaster; he also opened a tavern. Keeney followed him as postmaster from 1833 to 1847. In 1834, Keeney changed the name of the post office to Erie. Keeney was a justice of the peace in 1829, too.

Many areas around the neighborhood bore his name, such as the Keeney subdivision and Keeney Road. He was also involved with the development of a new port town called Havre, which ended up becoming Monroe's Atlantis (see the Havre section earlier in this chapter). Keeney passed away on March 9, 1847, still living at his original farm.

The first church in the county was built out of logs at Vienna in 1819; it would come to be known as St. Joseph's Erie. In 1826, a frame church replaced the log one and sufficed for over twenty-five years. In 1850, one of the area's first residents, Francis Cousino (Cousineau), donated twenty acres for a new church. The fine, large permanent brick church was completed in 1852 at 111 feet long by 47 feet wide. The first cemetery was St. Joseph's. There is also a Keeney Cemetery, called Pines Cemetery today, at Luna Pier Road between Telegraph and South Dixie Highway. It dates to 1847. The Keeney family set aside half an acre for it on a sandy knoll and always took care of it. Today, it is on private property.

Taverns and saloons dotted the landscape all around the county, but most were located by a thoroughfare or railroad. These resting places were eagerly anticipated travelers, who were often quite worn out by their long journey.

In Vienna, prior to 1840, a famous inn between Monroe and Toledo was Smith's Tavern, run by Ira Smith. It was located on the south side of Manhattan Road and West Dixie Highway. Another such establishment in Vienna was the Pioneer Roadside Tavern, which enjoyed popularity as a roadside inn. Passengers were so delighted with the tavern that they were often delayed in resuming their journey. Reasons for these delays ran the gamut from just needing rest to disabled or sick horses, coach repairs, accidents—you name it. Many such sojourns lasted overnight as the weary traveler—and stagecoach driver—enjoyed hot toddies, stick-to-your-ribs home cooking, plenty of libations, music, dancing and fellowship. It was not uncommon for drivers to have a hard time rounding up their passengers to resume the journey. The famous Frog Legg Inn at 2103 Manhattan Street was originally the Ross House (or Moross House), built in 1853 as a wooden clapboard house on a stone foundation. Through the years, it has transformed from a school to a butcher shop, a brothel, a tavern, a hotel and a favorite place for bootleggers during Prohibition. In 1944, it became the Frog Leg Inn, run by Tad and Catherine Cousino. A favorite stop in the early 1900s was the Vienna Junction Hotel on Vienna Road, east of Summit Street.

In November 1899, a strange train wreck took place in the vicinity. Passengers were stunned and shocked when suddenly it seemed that the

Town of Vienna (Erie). *Monroe Publishing Company.*

Frog Leg Inn (former Moross House), built 1853. *Author.*

AMI Central passenger train just fell into a ditch after it started bumping over the ties about two miles south of Vienna. The train was a complete tangled-up mess. The smoking car holding thirteen people was perched atop the engine, and the day coach was at a forty-five-degree angle dug into the embankment. The express car, filled with bulk oysters, was upside down in the ditch, and the parlor car was still upright but off the track entirely. The engineer, who was violently thrown out of the engine, managed to make his way back to the car to put the fire out, so there was no danger of the wreck catching fire.

A special train was dispatched from Detroit with doctors and medical supplies. It stopped in Monroe to pick up volunteers wanting to help. Another train was dispatched from Toledo as well and was the second to get there, after two hours. With forty people injured, a makeshift hospital had to be set up right away in the chair car. Passengers worked to help the injured as best they could. Yet against all odds, all but two people were able to make it to the hospital car without help.

As surprising as all this was, the biggest shock was yet to come, when division superintendent Sutherland said he thought the cause of the wreck might not have been an accident but rather a devious plan to wreck the train on purpose in order to rob it. The rails were examined, and it looked as if someone had purposely messed with it. It took no imagination to figure out what the tools of destruction were, since they had just been stolen from the Lake Shore tool shed at Vienna recently. The tools, a crowbar and a track wrench, were found lying by the tracks after the wreck. Oddly enough, no one recalled having seen any suspicious strangers in the village or by the tracks that day. However, resident Rudolph Morin said he saw two strangers in a field on his way to the wreck. He stopped them and asked them if anyone from the wreck was injured. But they did not return an answer and, instead, suddenly ran off as fast as they could across the field while Morin yelled after them.

Vienna is Erie today and has changed quite a bit. Some of the older structures and the Keeney house can still be seen. It is on the 1859 Geil map and in other maps up to the present under Erie.

Vienna Junction

Vienna Junction grew up along the Michigan Central (MC) railroad, just north of the Ohio line. It also served as the separation area for the MC and New York Central Toledo Division. It shows up on a 1936 and a 1941 map as Samaria.

Vistula

On the enchanting rise of a hill overlooking Swan Creek, with its deep and easily traversed channel, Vistula was born. It was situated next to the mouth of the Miami River near the home of Benjamin F. Stickney Esquire, who founded it along with Edward Bissell. It was an enchanting location for a new harbor town just inside the state line, about twenty miles from the village of Monroe. In 1832, a land company laid out the village of Vistula, and the Michigan Territorial Legislative Council approved a road to go through it.

In 1833, one E. Briggs opened a general store, and Lewis Goddard opened a dry goods store. Edward Bissell opened sawmill in July 1834. A post office was established on January 8, 1834, with Theodore Bissell as the first postmaster. It only lasted a year, however, and was closed on January 9, 1835. Later, a steam mill, a gristmill and a large iron foundry were established. After the Toledo War in 1836, the area was "forfeited to the government" by the Cincinnati Company and became part of Lucas County, Ohio. Today, the old village is part of the Vistula Historic District of Toledo and contains the oldest houses in the vicinity.

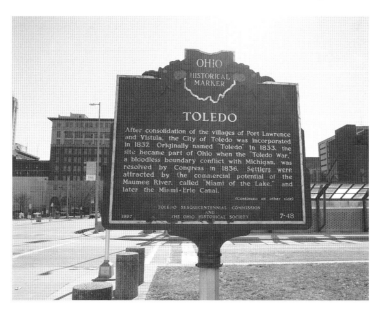

Toledo (Vistula) historical marker. *Author.*

Chapter 8

EXETER TOWNSHIP

EAST EXETER

East Exeter was a small community in the eastern section of Exeter Township. Its post office opened in 1845, with Peter Partlan as the first postmaster. Partlan owned property in the area, as shown on the 1859 Geil map. The post office ran for only eight months.

The area was served by the Long Bridge School, which was originally called the Stony Creek School before 1901. It was located at 10501 Finzel Road, just south of the bridge over South Stony Creek Road. It was originally wood but was rebuilt with brick in 1907. It ran until 1967, and today, it is a converted private residence. The school never changed locations, as evidenced by maps from 1859 up to the 1960s. There has been some confusion due to Lang's 1901 map, which seems to locate the school where a residence is at the corner of South Stony Creek and Finzel Roads. The confusion stems from the fact that the square representing the school is drawn on its actual location, but the label "school" appears where a house is represented by a square, off to the side. There was just not enough room to draw and write in such a small space. Whenever Lang drew a square to represent a school, he used a solid rectangle and then outlined it. So the school square is still drawn in the exact same place. The problem is that on a map, sometimes things are too condensed and can be misread.

In the 1890s, at just seventeen years old, Gertrude Golden taught at the school. She had about fifteen students in the fall, with most of the male

Long Bridge School (built circa 1907) today. *Author.*

students helping out on the farm. The males had to stay home on the farm to help out and thus did not attend school when it was harvest time. Gertrude was paid a handsome salary of twenty-five dollars a month and used part of it to board at Dickey's Boarding House, next to the Athlone Post Office.

One of East Exeter's most notable residents was Monroe entrepreneur and cofounder of Floral City Furniture Company Edwin J. Shoemaker, who would go on to design the first La-Z-Boy chair. He was born on June 2, 1907, to Louis and Mary (Zink) Shoemaker, who lived at 4300 Watson Road.

Unfortunately, in 1894, the peaceful community was rocked by a horrible scandal.

Joseph J. Geiermann was born on June 12, 1839, in Germany. He married Anna M. Zimmer on February 10, 1863, in Lorain, Ohio. They had nine children, one of whom was Henry J. Geiermann, who was born on February 6, 1867, in Lorain. The family moved to Exeter Township in 1880.

Henry married Agnes Weiss of Monroe on May 14, 1889. Agnes was born on January 28, 1866, in Monroe. At some point, they made their home in East Exeter Township, and Henry served as an Exeter Township

Above: Zink-Shoemaker cabin, circa 1898. *Monroe Publishing Company.*

Left: Agnes Geiermann tombstone, St. Patrick's Cemetery No. 2. *Author.*

officer. They had two children: a daughter, born in 1891, and a son, born in 1892. But after only five years of marriage, in 1894, their lives would change forever.

On February 28, 1894, twenty-eight-year-old Agnes Geiermann was found murdered in their East Exeter Township home. Henry claimed robbers broke into the house knowing that, as a township official, he had a large amount of money stored there. After stealing it, they killed the eyewitness—Agnes. But Henry soon found himself accused of the murder. He had a reputation as a hopeless gambler, and that did not help his case.

Henry immediately went to confession after the murder, but his confession could not be used at trial. The church members were in an uproar. The priest would not reveal what was said but did tell his congregation that when it came to their neighbor, they were "not to judge falsely."

At the first trial, Henry was acquitted. Agnes's body was exhumed from her grave in St. Patrick's Cemetery No. 2 on South Stony Creek and Exeter Roads and used as evidence in a second trial. Nonetheless, on December 1, 1898, the *Clinton Independent* reported that he was acquitted of the murder committed four years earlier and his friends heartily congratulated him in the courtroom with clapping and shouting.

Whether Henry was accused unjustly—as the verdicts seem to imply— or whether criminals were staking out the house for money and murdered Agnes, the horrific crime left two children, a two-year-old and a three-year-old, without their mother. Henry left the area and moved to North Dakota, where he died on June 25, 1910, at the age of forty-three. Agnes's murder was never solved.

There are no traces of East Exeter today; it is just part of Exeter Township, although the Long Bridge School is still there.

Exeter

The village of Exeter was named after its township and had a post office on Doty and South Stony Creek Roads from July 6, 1840, to June 28, 1842. The post office was restored on March 14, 1850, and ran until September 14, 1903. Henry Palmer was the first postmaster.

In 1859—as evidenced on the Geil map, section no. 7—there was a steam sawmill in Exeter. There was also a schoolhouse, called Herkimer School, which was built on the Herkimer family's land. It ran from 1859 to 1966 and is a private home today, located at 11777 Doty Road.

Scofield

Scofield was founded by Silas A. Scofield in 1873, after the Chicago & Canada Southern Railroad came through in 1872. A couple years later, in

1875, Charles Angerer settled in Scofield, opened a general store and started manufacturing charcoal and lumber.

In the early twentieth century, Theodore Drinkhahn ran the Scofield general store for eighteen years. He also served as the Exeter Township clerk.

In the winter of 1922, Scofield got a new creamery, which had an artificial ice plant run by a Mr. Simcox of Belleville. Also in the 1920s, Scofield got a new Methodist Episcopal church on the northwest corner of Scofield and Sumpter Roads.

The Scofield School, at Scofield and Jefferson Roads, opened in 1876 and was built out of wood. In 1961, a new block school with all modern facilities was built. Monroe entrepreneurs and founders of La-Z-Boy Chair Company cousins Edward Knabusch and Edwin Shoemaker were pupils at the Scofield School. In 1968, the school merged with Airport Schools. The building no longer exists, although behind the township hall is a schoolhouse. It is not Scofield School but McGowan School and was moved there in 2003 from Stout Road. The school was named after its first teacher, Agnes B. McGowan, and was built in 1888. It merged with Airport in 1996.

A notable event in Scofield was when thirty-year-old Nick R. Rinch was caught with a still in his vehicle in South Rockwood, on his way back home from Detroit. He was arrested and locked up in the county jail, to be charged with violating the liquor law.

Earl Miller, who lived in Scofield as a child, shared an unforgettable incident during an interview with his daughter Rebecca for her college history class. He told her that one of things he most remembered from his childhood was seeing the notorious John Dillinger. Dillinger was on the FBI's most wanted list as public enemy number one and was an infamous gangster. He and his gang robbed more than twenty-four banks in the Depression era.

Earl was hanging out at the general store with friends one night when a Ford Model A pulled up to get gas. As a woman filled up Dillinger's tank, he paced back and forth, and the only thing he said was, "How are you kids doing?" Earl says they had no idea who he was other than that he was dressed up in a suit. It was not until the next day, when the newspaper ran a story with a picture of him and the kind of stolen car he was riding in, that they understood who he was. Dillion was en route from Dundee; he stopped in Scofield and then went on to Carleton and Dearborn. Earl said had they known who he was, they would have been scared to death, because he was such a "notorious bank robber." Dillinger escaped from jail by making a pistol out of wood and jamming it into a guard's side.

Scofield exists as a village today and is composed of mostly houses. Some of the roads have since disappeared, as have industry and businesses. Scofield appeared on the 1876 Beers atlas and on other maps up through 1967 under Exeter.

WOOLMITH

Woolmith was a hamlet founded in 1894 about a mile from Scofield at Scofield and Doty Roads in Exeter Township by the Detroit, Toledo and Ironton Railroad. The railroad had a line that went directly into the quarry. The Woolmith Quarry was started in 1852 and known as the Michigan-Ohio Limestone Company. In 1913, it was bought by the Michigan Stone and Supply Company. Today, it is owned by Stoneco but across the road from the original quarry.

Woolsmith Store & Hotel, Scofield, circa 1900. *Monroe Publishing Company.*

Chapter 9

FRENCHTOWN TOWNSHIP

BREST

The area from the mouth of Stony Creek to Sandy Creek was an ideal location, by the water and next to Lake Erie. French Canadians started settling the area around 1810 and named it Brest after a seaport in Brest, France. Alexis Soleau, a farmer living at Sandy Creek, built the first gristmill in Monroe at Sandy Creek; he then built a large gristmill at Brest. His trade was carpentry, and he was also a millwright. But during the War of 1812 and the Battles of the River Raisin, both mills burned down, and he and his son Touissant were taken prisoner by the British and held at Fort Malden.

By 1826, there were about fourteen families living by the mouth of Stony Creek, and in 1836, a register of deeds was approved for the village plot of Brest in Frenchtown Township. The village got its own post office on July 15, 1836; Joseph Metcalf served as postmaster until July 8, 1863, when it was shut down. It was restored on February 28, 1890, and operated until August 15, 1903.

In 1837, H.S. Platt drew up a fancy map of the city with many businesses, charming homes, people lining the streets and a very appealing waterfront, with vessels lined up all along the copious docks. Platt was hoping to lure businesses to the town. Before long, it came to be called the "paper city" because there was nothing to back it up.

With Brest located close to Newport, a rivalry sprang up between the two settlements, fueled by each village's proprietor. Brest had H.S. Platt, while Newport had William White. Platt was definitely out of his league in that

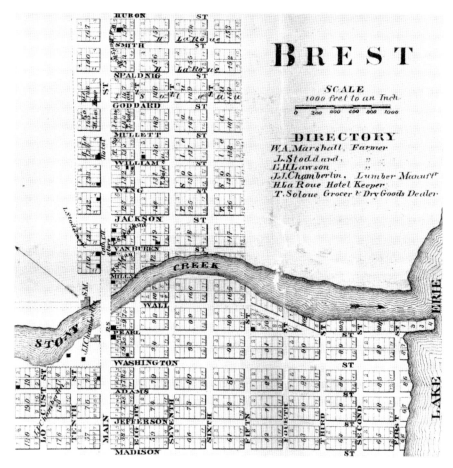

Brest, 1859 Geil map. *Library of Congress.*

he was the financial manager of the Bank of Brest, while William White was pretty much a one-man show in Newport: he was postmaster, notary public and justice of the peace, and he ran the hotel and store. But Platt was not deterred. He had the following advertisement published in the *Monroe Advocate* on February 14, 1837:

> *Jobs to Let at Brest—The proprietors of the town of Brest wish to contract for the erecting of a large and spacious four story building for a Public house, to be built on the most approved plan for convenience and elegance. Said house to be built of wood, the size on the ground to be in proportion to the height. Those wishing to take the job will please furnish the subscriber at Monroe with a plan and cost of building the same. The lumber and*

materials can all be obtained at Brest. Likewise to let, the building of a dwelling house, all materials furnished. A plan will be given when called upon.…Brick makers would do well to commence the manufacture of brick at Brest, as good clay and sand can be obtained near together, and a ready market for any quantity of brick.

The rivalry was set to play out in the newspaper now. William White had the following bluffing ad put in the paper the following week, on March 28, 1837, right underneath Platt's:

Jobs to Let at Newport—The proprietor of the town of Newport wishes to contract for the erection of a large and spacious fifteen story building for a public house, to be built on the most approved plan for convenience and elegance. Said house to be built of marble; the site on the ground to be in proportion to the height. Those wishing to take the Job will please furnish the subscriber with a plan and cost of building the same. Also, to let, the building of twenty or thirty dwelling houses; all materials furnished, with a plan of each.

Platt was determined to answer White's farce and thus loaded up all the burly men of the village in a sleigh and headed toward his rival. But White caught wind of the planned visit and prepared to meet his nemesis with a barrel of wine and all kinds of homemade delights. Both men were in jovial spirits, appreciating each other's cunning. A good time was had by all, and the hatchet was buried from then on.

The "paper city" of Brest also had a "paper bank," if you will, run by Platt. Although the bank was brick and mortar, its contents were not. "Wildcat banks" were not uncommon at this time. A wildcat bank actually has no assets to back it up but issues its own worthless currency nonetheless.

Knowing an inspection was coming, the bank had to borrow money from resident Lewis Goddard. The money was deposited the day before, and the day after the inspection, it was returned to Goddard. But the inspectors grew wise to the scheme and came back unannounced the following week for a surprise visit. The bank was caught with only $138.39 on hand.

Despite all Platt's work to encourage settlement, the reality of Brest in 1850 was nothing like his proposed plan. There was only one large hotel, one store and his wildcat bank. Eventually, however, the village did grow to contain a township hall, a school, a church, a cemetery, a tavern, a fishery, a tobacco factory and a brick factory.

Brest Village School, built 1927. *Author.*

The first school, called Brest Village School, was located in the township hall on North Dixie Highway and shows up on the 1859 Geil map. In the 1876 Beers atlas, it appears at its second location, 3684 Brest Road. Then, in 1927, a new school was built just behind the second one. The second one became a grocery store for a while. The third school was used until 1953, and today, it is a privately owned church.

Gertrude Golden, who taught at Brest Village School, said the pupils liked to skate out to Brest Bay during recess in the winter, especially around 1899 when, about a mile from the school, a large freighter sank. Then, in the spring it floated back up again. It was reported on January 17, 1950, that "about 200 yards North of the Monroe channel...lie the remains of this approximately 60-foot schooner, believed to be 'Cap' Dandron's three masted lumbar schooner, the Vernia M. Blake. The double-planked craft, with heavy wooden stakes of still stout lumbar, had a 15-foot stern. She succumbed to a storm about 1898, when heading for refuge at the Monroe Piers."

Like most lost towns, Brest had a cemetery, too. It was located just west of North Dixie Highway on North Stony Creek Road, right by the banks of

Stony Creek. No one seems to know how many people were buried there, since no records were kept, but it contained one of the earliest residents of the area, a Revolutionary War soldier by the name of Gideon Badger. Gideon passed away on April 3, 1826. The locals contend that a man by the name of Frank Walker, who lived there, collected the tombstones that used to be in the cemetery and used them as steps to the cellar of his house. The 1901 Lang map shows Frank Walker living at that location or perhaps next to it. The house burned down at some point, and another house was built there by Herb Sisung (or Susing). Today, the cemetery is an open field by the banks of the creek once again—but with no evidence of it ever having existed in the first place.

The surname Dewey became synonymous with Brest. In fact, there is a Dewey Road in Brest today. Jesse N. Dewey came to Brest in 1864 with his son, John McMartin Dewey, and opened a fishing business. Sturgeon was abundant, and the family shipped fish all over the country. In the 1880s, the eggs went all the way to Europe and were relabeled and shipped back as Russian caviar. American caviar could not be given away, but when it was relabeled "Russian" and shipped back, it was considered a delicacy and fetched a high price. The Deweys sold fish, especially sturgeon, to peddlers, who in turn sold them as food. The Deweys also owned an icehouse in Brest where they kept the fish. They hired help seasonally and provided them with room and board as well as paying them a wage. Incidentally, the Dewey house was rumored to have been a station on the Underground Railroad.

The Dewey brothers, Joseph B. and Jesse N., were very successful at starting their own fisheries; they eventually ended up controlling most of the fishing in Monroe County, with docks at Toledo and Detroit. Eventually, they even shipped to places as far away as Colorado. The brothers bought up lakefront property to extend their holdings and made good use of steamers and tugs for shipping. They ended up employing up to fifty people.

Another name synonymous with Brest was Dr. Amy Phillipart from Detroit. He became something of a local celebrity. When he came to town, around 1917, his automobile got stuck in the deep mud just north of the bridge at Brest. Resident Irving Sisung took his team of horses up to the bridge to help pull him out. The doctor explained to Sisung that he was going to settle down in Brest and was looking for a piece of property—but he was going to buy the first piece of property he saw with a dog running across it. Once his car was free, he headed across the bridge and turned left onto Pearl Drive. Suddenly, he saw a little yellow dog run across the road and north across a field to the creek. So, true to his word, that was the land he bought. He became known as a faith healer by praying and laying on of hands. He was called the "human X-ray" because he could "see right through" a person, instinctively figuring out what was wrong with them. He charged little for his services, and for the poor, he charged nothing. As his reputation grew, people poured into Brest to see him; at one time, they were lined up for a whole block waiting their turn.

During Prohibition, Brest was front and center, since it was right in the heart of the rum-running area. Residents were bothered by rumrunners banging down their doors, offering large sums of money to store their liquor. Irving Sisung's family remembered how one year, the lake was frozen solid, and the figures coming across the ice from Canada looked like flocks of bluebirds flying in from everywhere. The family was especially fearful when one night, at two o'clock, they heard a terrible crashing sound and, looking out the window, saw a car upside down in their yard. Inside was a Mr. Blanchett, a bootlegger from one of the beach areas. He had been shot dead. There was no liquor in the car, just many empty bags. It was said Blanchett was killed by another bootlegger, but the case was never solved.

Today, little remains of Brest: the school, a few old houses and that is about it. Even many of the roads have ceased to exist. Brest shows up on the 1859 Geil map and appears on some other maps up to about 1967 or so.

Loranger

Loranger was a settlement named after the Edward Loranger family. Edward, born in 1796, migrated from Quebec and made his way to Frenchtown around 1816, where he built many commercial buildings along the River Raisin. In 1822, Loranger built a sawmill and then, in 1825, built his house along Stony Creek. The sawmill was located east of Old Plank Road (current Telegraph Road) on the creek. He went on to open a gristmill on the creek in 1828 after his marriage to Marianne Navarre, with whom he had five children. The red gristmill was different than other mills, however, because he built it to grind not only corn but wheat as well. He used an advanced process run by conveyor belts and buckets that was invented by Oliver Evans in the late 1780s. Edward dammed up Stony Creek for his mills; Stony Creek was much larger and deeper than it is today, and the local kids could swim in it. The mills proved to be valuable assets to the community.

Loranger Mill, Stony Creek. *Monroe County Library System.*

The village of Loranger received a post office on January 16, 1865, and it ran until April 26, 1869, with Joel J. Dussean as the first postmaster. Loranger School was developed in the late 1800s and was located on the crossroads of North Monroe, North Telegraph and South Stony Creek Roads. But after 1876 and before 1901, it was rebuilt near the corner of South Stony Creek and Stumpmier Roads (which, back then, came together). Its name was changed to Mill School from 1912 to 1915, then to Dam School from 1915 to 1932 and back to Loranger from 1932 to 1948, when it merged with Airport Schools. Today, it is a private residence at 7119 South Stony Creek Road.

When Edward Loranger passed away in 1887, his son Joseph Loranger inherited the mills. Joseph had no end of troubles when residents complained in 1892 that the dam, which had been there since 1824, was backing up the water for five to six miles and creating a four-thousand-acre wasteland that was utterly useless and stank something awful. Despite being offered $500 to demolish the dam, Joseph Loranger would not budge and was called "stubborn" numerous times. Although he managed to get through this ordeal, this was not the end of his troubles.

Joseph ended up going to court in 1921 over the relocation and paving of the Old Plank Road (Telegraph today). Part of his property was needed to relocate the road at the point where the bridge went over Stony Creek.

Phantom Bridge, Telegraph Road. *Author.*

Former Edward Loranger homestead today. *Author.*

Over the years, however, Joseph would not play ball and refused to give up his land for the relocation. Three Monroe commissioners went to the property to personally view it. They were appointed by the circuit court in the condemnation proceedings of the Monroe County Board of Road Commissioners against Joseph Loranger. After visiting the property, the commissioners decided to condemn the nine-tenths of an acre needed for the relocation and awarded Joseph $250 for the acreage and damages.

Shortly after this, in 1922, Joseph Loranger passed away and passed on the mills to his adopted son, Clarence Lemerand. Lemerand had barely inherited them when someone attempted to blow up the dam under the cover of darkness around eleven o'clock on May 24, 1923. The result was a six-foot gaping hole in the dam. Clarence sold the gristmill to Henry Ford in 1926. The mill was moved in 1928 and is currently on exhibit at the Henry Ford Museum in Greenfield Village. The Loranger house can still be seen at 7211 South Stony Creek Road. The old "ghost bridge" and remnants of old Telegraph Road are still apparent as well. Loranger first shows up in the 1876 Beers atlas, then under Stony Point on maps up to about 1942.

Meyer (Stony Creek, Matteson)

Meyer was first known as Stony Creek and, for a time, as Matteson. It started as a station on the Michigan Central and the Lakeshore and Michigan Southern Railroad and is located at North Stony Creek Road by Mentel Road. The village was renamed Meyer when Charles J. Meyer served as the first postmaster, in 1899; the post office ran until 1903. Charles also ran a store in Meyer. The Meyer homestead was located on North Stony Creek Road and was mentioned in the *Monroe Evening News* in the 1920s. There was another store owned by H. Renner and also a creamery. On the corner of Stony Creek and Mental Roads was the Stony Creek School, started in 1859. At one point, it became Meyers School, and in 1948, it merged with Jefferson Schools. The village named Meyer can be seen on the 1901 Lang map.

Sandy Creek

Sandy Creek was a village founded around 1780 or so by French Canadians who settled in the area. The creek actually starts in London Township and flows down to Lake Erie, but the village was located right off the mouth of Lake Erie. Speculators from outside Monroe County, such as Meldrum and Parks, operated a gristmill on the creek.

Only a few dozen people ever settled in the area because it was cut short by the War of 1812. The subsequent Battles of the River Raisin fought in January 1813 were a devastating loss to the Americans. As a result, many of the settlers abandoned the area. A historical marker at William C. Sterling State Park reads, in part:

> The small settlement was founded as early as 1780 by the French shortly before the much larger Frenchtown settlement, which was founded in 1784 just south near the River Raisin. At the time, the area was under the administration of the British Province of Quebec and predated American territorial control. In 1787, the area became part of the newly established American Northwest Territory, then briefly into the Indiana Territory in 1800, and finally into the Michigan Territory in 1805.

The first Battle of the River Raisin, fought on January 18, 1813, was an American victory, after the battle, many of the Native warriors (who fought for the British) were forced to retreat a few miles to the north. As they were passing through Sandy Creek, young inhabitant Jean-Baptiste Solo started mocking them, asking if they were running from the Kentuckians, who fought on the American side. Unfortunately for him, the answer to his question was a gunshot and a bullet that met its mark. Although he was mortally wounded, he managed to make it to the house of his father-in-law, René LeBeau. He was yelling as he got there that he had been shot. When Rene opened the door, Jean-Baptiste fell into his arms and died within minutes. René screamed to his two youngest children to run upstairs and hide. René had barely laid Jean-Baptiste on the bed when he heard the Natives approach the front door. He ran to the window, peeked out and, recognizing some of the Potawatomi, opened the door. This was a fatal mistake, however. As he opened the door, they fired on him, killing him instantly. His adult son, Etienne, immediately ran to the door, pushing it shut on one of the warriors' arms. When the Native freed his arm, Etienne quickly bolted the door. To Etienne's surprise, the Natives turned around and left the house.

Etienne figured they had no time to waste, they needed to get to safety so he yelled to his fourteen-year-old sister Genevieve and eight-year-old brother Alexis to come down right away. He explained that they would have to escape two miles to the Frenchtown settlement. Not taking time to grab anything, the children took off running barefoot through the deep snow as fast as they could. But they had not gotten far when they heard gunshots being fired in their direction. In terror, they ran faster through the darkness; the younger ones outran their older brother until they reached Frenchtown at dawn. The settlers could not believe what they heard from the lips of the young children, whose feet were raw and bloody from their ordeal.

Although it would always remain a small settlement, later, the Sandy Creek School and a church were built. The school was built around 1865 and shows up on the 1876 Beers atlas, located at the corner of North Dixie Highway and Hurd Road. In 1950, the school and property were auctioned off. Sandy Creek Mission started off as a log building, then was rebuilt with a wood frame. There was an altar inside of it that was later auctioned off. Sandy Creek resident and farmer Peter Suzor lived at 2293 North Sandy Creek Road and was a township officer numerous times. Just like the school and the church, there are no remains of his home today.

Clearance Durocher grew up in Sandy Creek and remembers all the fantastic duck, goose and pheasant hunting. He went to school at the Sandy Creek School in the late 1800s. He said there were forty to fifty students in the school. When his father died, when Clearance was thirteen, he had to focus on running the farm for his mother and two sisters and rarely attended school. That was the case with many a young man who had to help on the family farm, especially in the warm months.

Clearance became an adept horse catcher, as runaway horses were pretty common in those days—especially after the advent of the automobile. He says there were many horse-and-buggy accidents involving automobiles because the autos scared the horses, especially in the city.

There were milk houses throughout the hamlet, to which milk was brought from the barn to cool down. Ice was needed for the milk houses, and there were icehouses for storing the ice, too. But since the creek was so small, it was hard to collect ice there, and the settlers had to go to Stony Creek to hack off big enough chunks of ice. Then the ice would be packed in sawdust to keep it cool in the shed. It would last all summer because the sawdust was an insulator. Ice was necessary back then to keep food and milk cold so it would not spoil.

There is nothing left of the hamlet but the road, the creek itself and the historical marker at William Clarke Sterling State Park.

Scrabble Hollow

Scrabble Hollow is located on War Road. The story of how Scrabble Hollow got its name came from Irish settlers in the area. One day, farmer Jake Renner got his carriage stuck in the mud while trying to cross the creek. He became so agitated that he started whipping his horses and whooping and hollering so loudly he scared them to death, and they proceeded to "scrabble" around him and run as fast as they could to get out of there. Thus, the name Scrabble Hollow was born.

Another legend comes from local author Gertrude Golden, who attended the Scrabble Hollow School when she was young. She said that the creek was "scrabby"—in other words, winding all over the place—and the area was named after the creek, which was wide enough for the children to skate on at recess and originated from a marsh located off to the east. The creek became known as the Scrabble Hollow Creek.

The Scrabble Hollow School, across the street from Renner, is at 8186 War Road after Buhl Road. It was originally wooden and built around the 1870s.

Former Scrabble Hollow School, built 1898. *Author.*

It was rebuilt with brick in 1898 and closed in 1948, when it consolidated with Airport Schools. Today, it is a private residence.

There existed a Scrabble Hollow Telephone Company in 1910, with landowner Louis Yoas as the president. On September 27, 1922, companies were given the opportunity to bid on deepening and widening the Scrabble Hollow Creek.

Scrabble Hollow shows up in a map of Stony Point from 1936 to 1967.

STEINER

Not much is known about William Steiner, who founded the settlement in 1873. There is only one reference to him in Buckley's *History of Monroe County*. It states that Charles Angerer of Scofield purchased William Steiner's sawmill in Exeter Township. The other William Steiner was a hardware store owner in the city of Monroe at the time.

In any case, the settlement was around the intersection of Steiner and Laduke Roads. It started as a railroad depot for the Flint & Pierre Marquette Railroad. The railroad crossing at South Stony Creek in Steiner is where many of the trains stopped to take on wood and water. A post office opened

Steiner Inn. *Monroe County Library System.*

Steiner Basket Factory. *Monroe County Library System.*

on September 7, 1886, and operated until July 31, 1925, with John Kohler as the first postmaster.

The town had the William Steiner & Sons hardware store and the LaDuke general store, run by Paul LaDuke, which sold everything, including liquor. There was a creamery and a saloon right in it. Edgar R. Calkins moved to Steiner with his family in 1876, when he was thirteen years old. Seventeen years later, he ended up running a sawmill and making bushel and market baskets. He would take orders for the baskets and make them to certain specifications. They were so popular that he ended up shipping them out to places like New York and Pennsylvania. Fruit and vegetable baskets were made by hand, mostly by family members and a handful of others. The baskets cost thirty-five cents a dozen for small ones and a dollar a dozen for larger ones.

There was also the Steiner Inn, a granary, a pickle factory, freight scales, a pottery and brickworks and a schoolhouse. The Asam School was built on the property of Peter Asam. It shows up on the 1859 Geil map at Toben and South Stony Creek Roads. In 1881, a new school was built just a little farther down on South Stony Creek; it was used until 1959, when it was closed. Today, it is no longer there.

A sad incident in the town's history took place on May 3, 1948, when a tremendous fire broke out. It managed to engulf many buildings and the general store. But the saddest part was that it claimed two lives, those of seventy-year-old Margaret Gibson and five-year-old Magadline Moyer. The closest fire department was five miles away, and it was too late to help the woman and the child. This fact led to the 1949 development of the Frenchtown Township Volunteer Fire Department.

Once the trains no longer carried passengers to Steiner and no one was stopping there anymore, the town significantly declined and had disappeared by the 1940s. Today, the only remnants of the once-thriving village are a few houses and the name Steiner Road.

Although the Asam School shows up on the 1859 Geil map, Steiner itself does not show up until 1896 on the Ogle map and is shown up until about 1967 on other Monroe Township maps.

Stony Creek (Rocky River)

Before there was a settlement at Stony Creek, an extensive mill and some other businesses were already in operation around 1810, prior to the Battles of the River Raisin in January 1813. During the battles, however, the mill and other buildings were set afire and destroyed. The actual village of Stony Creek grew up in the 1830s alongside the creek about four miles upstream from the mouth of the River Raisin and along the crossover of the Detroit and Toledo Shoreline Railroad (D&TSL). A post office operated briefly from July 6, 1840, to January 18, 1841, with Patrick Collins as the first postmaster. Businesses and a large mill were already running alongside the stream before many people came there, and the high, dry banks of creek encouraged settlement. Eventually, fourteen families made Stony Creek their home.

Anytime during the year, you could see Native Americans hunting and fishing all along Stony Creek. Sometimes they would beg for food from the settlers but never caused any issues, and they coexisted peacefully.

As in many early towns, roads were noticeably bad, especially in the winter, with ice, snow and rain. Wagon wheels would get ten inches of mud caked on them and horses could not pull the weight. The snow was so deep that farmers used their fields more than the roads to get through.

The village had a lumber mill and a creamery where the farmers could bring their milk, usually in ten-gallon cans, and put it in a large vat to be separated. The creamery owner would then pay the farmers for their cream. There was also a lumber mill, where the farmers could take the wood from cutting down their trees to the mill and have it cut to specific measurements in order to build their houses or other buildings.

Monrod LaPrad ran a cider mill called LaPrad's Cider Mill or Cider Mill Farm; it was located on War Road by North Stony Creek Road.

The 1859 Geil map refers to the area as Stony Creek Station, but at the turn of the century, the area became known as Meyer (please refer to "Meyer" under Frenchtown Township). Meyers School was located at Mentel and Stony Creek Roads. It was renamed Stony Creek School after 1902. It shows up on the 1859 Geil map and continued at the same location until it closed in 1950.

No remnants of the village exist today, other than a few houses.

Chapter 10

IDA TOWNSHIP

FEDERMAN (MONROE JUNCTION)

This town was originally known as Monroe Junction; its name was changed to Federman because confusion between Monroe Junction and the city of Monroe. Federman was named after a family who lived there (as was the case with many such towns)—specifically John Federman, a German immigrant who settled with his wife, Caroline, in the area in 1851. He ended up working at the depot for thirty years.

Starting in 1884, the Toledo, Ann Arbor, Northern Michigan Railroad and the Lake Shore and Michigan Southern Railroad crossing was at Federman. The Lake Shore goes all the way back to 1839 and, at the time, was the only railroad that ran from east to west traversing Monroe County all the way to Adrian. When it intersected the Ann Arbor line, Federman was born. Dozens of passengers loaded and unloaded at the Federman depot daily; it was called "traveler central." Some accounts say as many as one hundred passengers traversed the depot per day from the areas of Ann Arbor, Adrian, Bell Isle, Toledo and Monroe. One account in the newspaper said: "Federman is getting to be quite the town. It has two telephone lines, two railroads, and all that is lacking are the electric cars." With so much activity at the junction, it was not surprising that every now and then, an accident occurred, such as a derailment that happened in 1915.

The main street was Haines Road, connected by Albian Road on the south and Ida West Road to the north. A post office was established on

Former Federman School, built 1872. *Author.*

June 22, 1899, and operated until August 31, 1906, with Jay Bates as the first postmaster. The hamlet contained a general store, a cider mill and a school, as well as about fifteen family farms.

Federman School was built in 1872 at 13340 Ida West Road and in 1946 became part of Ida Schools; today, it is a private residence. Eda Schultz, born in 1899, remembered walking three miles to go to school there all the way up through the eighth grade; she also remembers taking the train from the Fetterman Depot to the fair up in Adrian.

Federman had quite the local legend: residents said that compasses would not work there and claimed the settlement was immune to severe storms and tornados. Unfortunately, it was not immune to the criminal activity that was witnessed in 1837.

Federman and nearby Lulu were embroiled in quite the crime story in 1837. It thrust Monroe, as well as these little towns, into the spotlight. It all started in Detroit when two gunmen kidnapped a used car salesman, Fred Williams. The men proceeded to drive him to Toledo, Ohio, and left him there tied to a tree. The men planned to head back to Detroit in Williams's farm truck. They were not counting on a police blockade set up around Monroe, however.

Alcide "Frenchy" Benoit was a twenty-four-year-old blacksmith from Detroit who was originally born in Canada. He had already done time in prison for stealing and concealing weapons. In the Michigan State Reformatory in Ionia, he met felon John H. "Smitty" Smith from Flint, and they quickly became friends.

Michigan state troopers Richard F. Hammond and Sam S. Sineni were on the lookout for the two renegades. Hammond, only twenty-six years old, was engaged and had only served for eighteen months. Sineni was the same age and had been a trooper for about two years; he was also a newlywed.

The troopers had no idea their whole lives were about to change when they caught up with the fugitives in Monroe shortly before midnight on January 19, 1937. According to Frenchy's own confession, the troopers stopped the pair in the stolen truck in Monroe and proceeded to separate them. Hammond managed to get Frenchy into his squad car, while Sineni took control of Smitty in the stolen vehicle. But it was not long before Hammond lost control of the situation when Frenchy produced a hidden revolver, and according to Frenchy:

> As the car started, I jammed the gun into the officer's rib and told him to slow down. Instead, Hammond started to go faster so I slugged him over the eye with the butt of my pistol and told him to turn onto a side road. The other officer behind came up close. I turned around and fired three shots. When I started shooting Hammond said he was going to crash the car and I told him if he did, I'd kill him sure. Then the other car went into a ditch and I stopped. I was going to take my partner away from the other cop, but a truck blocked the way, so I made Hammond drive down lonely roads until we came where I left him.

After making Hammond stop, Frenchy said he "then got out and put one of the handcuffs on his [Hammond's] wrists. When I tried to get him out of the car, he put up a fight and we rolled over on the ground. I could see he was getting the best of me, then I fired during the scuffle and he got limp. I cuffed his hands around the post on the mail box."

After leaving Hammond, Frenchy found himself pursued by two Monroe deputies, and a desperate situation unfolded as the cars dashed through the streets of Monroe County for ten miles, swerving back and forth as gunshots went hurtling through the air. Frenchy finally crashed into a ditch and ran out on foot into the woods. In the patrol car, the deputies did not find

Hammond but, instead, his bloodstained uniform coat. Finally, around five o'clock in the morning, other officers in the area came upon Hammond's body—slumped over a rural postal box, with his wrists bound by his own handcuffs. He had been shot in the head.

After fleeing on foot through the sleet-covered dirt, Frenchy sought refuge in a barn in Federman. After dark, he walked up to the Balog farmhouse and threatened the fifty-five-year-old father, Paul, and his sixteen-year-old son, Steve. Steve later said, "My dad and I started to walk out the driveway with Benoit, but we hadn't gone 100 feet when he pulled out two guns. 'If you don't want to get killed drive me to Monroe,' he said." Paul's suspicious thirteen-year-old daughter Anna was determined to let the police know what had happened, despite her mother's pleas not to go. Anna set out in the frigid, ice-filled air, clasping a lantern in her hand as she made her way to the next farmhouse, that of Irvin Karns. Anna later said, "When they drove away, I grabbed my lantern and started up the road to the Karns' place." There, she was able to alert police to the situation. Because of her tenacity, Frenchy was caught by four troopers about three miles outside of Monroe.

Former Federman Depot at Monroe County Fairgrounds. *Author.*

They managed to pursue him onto a side road and fired into the hood of the truck, causing it to stop. Frenchy got out and threw his hands up in the air, saying, "You've got me, coppers! Yes, I'm the guy."

In terms of the number of officers involved, the crime was one of the largest in Michigan's history, with over three hundred officers from Michigan, Ohio and Indiana participating. It was widely reported in the media, and thus some details of the story are muddled. But there is no doubt that once Frenchy was caught, he was heavily guarded, as the people of Monroe were angry and out for justice after the events that had just unfolded. Eventually, Frenchy was sentenced to life in prison and hard labor after being charged with first degree murder and numerous other crimes. Frenchy ended up dying of cancer in prison in 1951.

Today, nothing exists of Federman; the track is still there, passing through the countryside but no longer hauling passengers. The depot was moved to the Monroe County Fairgrounds and serves as the Little Smoky fair train ticket booth. Federman shows up on the 1896 Ogle map and on other maps up through 1941, under Dundee.

Harwick

The Harwick family lived in the area in the 1920s; thus, it appears the hamlet was named after them. Harwick School shows up on the 1859 Geil map, just north of the Tunnicliffe and Kruse Roads intersection. But on the 1876 atlas, it appears across the street on the south side of Tunnicliffe Road and was apparently rebuilt at some point. Lastly, on the 1901 Lang map, it appears to have relocated and been rebuilt again at the northwest corner of Morocco and Secor Roads. It closed in 1947 and is a private residence today.

Lulu

In 1853, Henry Y. West bought forty acres in what became Lulu along Douglas and Lulu Road. The name's origin is not known, but it may have belonged to an early settler's daughter. Another rumor has it that the first supervisor of Ida had two daughters, Ida and Lulu, each of whom he named a town after. But more than likely, the name came from the daughter of Governor Ashley of Toledo, who was involved in getting the Toledo and

Main street of Lulu, 1909. *Monroe County Library System, Ida.*

Ann Arbor Railroad depot into Lulu in the first place, in 1872. A post office was established on June 29, 1880, and ran until July 15, 1941, with Paul Nill as the first postmaster; he was also a storekeeper.

The community had a couple general stores, a hardware store, a barbershop, a pickle factory, a creamery, many coal yards, a school, two churches, a cemetery, a quarry and, later, the Greener Hall. The Greener Hall held dances and box socials, where the single women would make up a box containing chicken and pie, fancily decorated. The boxes would be auctioned off and the winner would get to share them with the female cook. Later, the Greener Hall burned down.

Many of the farmers in the area grew sugarcane to make into sorghum. Sorghum was made by chopping up sugarcane, then running it through the rollers at the mill to squeeze all the juice out. Then the juice was put into flat pans about eight inches deep, six feet wide and twenty feet long; a fire was put under the pans; and the juice was boiled down to the desired consistency and sweetness. There was a cider mill in Federman where one could get sugarcane ground.

Resident Burt Dutcher would peddle around town with his horse and wagon, selling cider, kerosene and other goods. He did this for years and was always well supplied with a large variety of items, which he stored in

Lulu Creamery, 1909. *Monroe County Library System, Ida.*

his barn. In the 1920s, he ran the general store and was postmaster. As with most such towns, the post office was located inside the store.

One night, Dutcher got quite the surprise when he awoke to his dog incessantly barking at two o'clock in the morning. He was sleeping in the back of the store, where he stayed, when he was startled awake by the loud barking coming from the front of the store. When he got up to investigate, he was shocked to see the front door swinging open and the seven-hundred-pound safe sitting outside on the ground in front of the post office. He heard tires screeching outside and saw a large automobile circling around and speeding off. Looking at the open door, he realized just what had happened. Burglars had pried open the front door and tried to make off with the seven-hundred-pound safe. But just as they were trying to load it into the car, the dog's blaring howls suddenly penetrated the air and, evidently, scared them out of their wits—and they dropped the safe, ran and sped off. The $700 in cash was saved, and the dog was hailed a hero.

The Lulu School shows up on the 1876 Beers atlas, as does the cemetery. The land for the schoolhouse was leased for ninety-nine years. In 1919, the school became known as the Moyer City School. On the 1901 Lang map, the Lulu United Baptist and Lulu Methodist Churches show up. Today, the Methodist church still exists at 12810 Lulu Road.

The Lulu Cemetery became known as the Ida Township Cemetery, located on Lulu Road, west of Douglas Road. The earliest grave dates to 1855 and is still there today. There is also a grave in the cemetery without

Former Lulu School today. *Author.*

an occupant, that of Ezra Younglove. Ezra Younglove served in the War of 1812 as chief gunner for Oliver Hazard Perry on the Niagara in the Battle of Lake Erie on September 10, 1813. He received a gold medal from the State of Kentucky for his valiant conduct in the battle. He was also a spy during the same war. According to his wishes, he was buried at the county's poor farm, Potter's Field. Today, that cemetery is on the grounds of the Monroe County Community College on South Raisinville Road. In his last years, Younglove lived in Lulu with his relatives. Although they agreed to his wish to be buried at Potter's Field, they later wanted to honor him with a tombstone. Today, that tombstone is in the West family plot in the Lulu Cemetery, although Younglove's remains are still at Potter's Field.

Not many towns recognized the occupation of the undertaker, but it was a necessary trade, especially back then with all the epidemics, such as smallpox and cholera. Often, the township would procure the hearse carriage—and sometimes the horse, too—and keep it at the township hall. Farmers usually made the casket, and neighbors would bring food for the funeral. There was a three-day period of mourning. The corpse was never left alone, so someone had to stay up all night with it. Every so often, it would be rubbed down with a liquid to help preserve the body. Sometimes young people would sit up with the corpse and make a regular party of the affair. No drinking was allowed but high spirits were.

In the town of Lulu, the undertaker in deed, but not necessarily in name, was H.Y. West. He was quite the local character, of advanced age, who was summoned whenever the need arose. He would carry his "cooling-off board" where he laid out the body and took measurements. Then he would go back to his shop, which was in the back of his house facing the quarry. He would make the coffin and often do the service, too. He was the one everyone called on if someone died from a dreaded disease or epidemic of the time, because no one wanted to have anything to do with the body. In Lulu, the greatly feared disease that swept through the area was called the black measles, and it claimed the lives of three children in the same family. Today, we know it as Rocky Mountain spotted fever, a bacterial disease spread by a tick bite. It causes a dark, blackish-looking rash on the skin.

There is a quarry in Lulu that has a depression of five acres and is nine feet deep. In 1896, it filled up with water but managed to empty itself in only three days—which stunned the residents, as that never happened before. There are many depressions throughout the area. Rumor has it that long ago, a man riding his horse sank down through the dirt into one of these sinkholes and was never seen again.

Lulu today. *Author.*

Remains of Lulu railroad depot. *Author.*

Lulu was quite the town in its heyday, but today, little remains. There are the remnants of the train depot, the moved schoolhouse, the church and a few houses. It shows up on the 1896 Ogle map and up through 1972 on other maps under Ida.

MAPLE GROVE

Little is known about Maple Grove. The L.J. Ostrander family built their home, and the hamlet grew up around it. In 1915, it was reported in the newspaper that the Maple Grove Church was transformed into a Sunday school. There was also a Maple Grove Cemetery in 1919.

The Ruettinger family donated land for a school, and a Mr. Finn was the first school board officer. The name Finn was adopted for the school until 1931, when it became known as the Maplegrove School. On the 1859 Geil map, the school is on Lulu Road, just west of the corner with Geiger Road. In 1880, it was rebuilt at 4599 Geiger Road, and it closed in 1945. Today, it is a private residence.

MOROCCO (SEOLA)

Morocco, which was originally Seola, has an unclear history. We know that in 1866, John Porter opened up a mercantile business in Seola. Also, in 1878, Seola was a station for the Toledo and Ann Arbor Railroad. Morocco got its post office in 1884, with John Griner as the first postmaster. Business owner John Porter was postmaster in 1886, and the post office ran until 1906.

The post office was located at the intersection of Morocco and Jackman Roads, as was a church and the Morocco School. The school was built in 1875 and eventually merged with Ida Schools in 1946. Today, the school is a church.

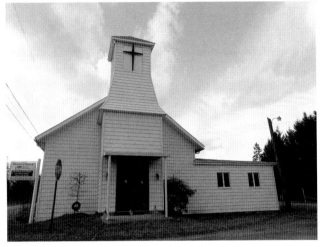

Top: Former Morocco Church today. *Author.*

Bottom: Former Morocco School today. *Author.*

Life was not easy for a student living in the first quarter of the twentieth century. D. Gere, who lived in Morocco as a child on a two-hundred-acre farm, remembered that first thing in the morning he had to milk the cows, feed the horses, do his farm chores, eat breakfast and then walk a mile and a half to the schoolhouse in Morocco. Once school was out, he had to walk home again, milk the cows again, clean the horse stables and feed the horses again.

Updates about Morocco were given in the *Monroe Evening News* in the 1920s. Morocco first shows up on the 1896 Ogle map and under "Dundee" on maps up through 1972.

RICHARDSON

Richardson was founded in the mid-1880s, largely by German settlers. The Joseph Richardson family came to the area in 1842, and Joseph bought his farm at 6380 Geiger Road from John H. Converse in 1846. He soon donated land for a cemetery to be located not far from the rear of his house. He also donated land for a school to be built across the street. The log school

Former Joseph Richardson homestead today. *Author.*

Richardson Cemetery. *Author.*

was built sometime between 1850 and 1860. At some point, it was replaced by a brick school, and it was consolidated with Ida in 1946. The old school caught fire in 1951, the night before it was to close permanently. Joseph also donated land for a Methodist Episcopal church.

Today, the house and farm as well as the cemetery can still be seen at 6380 Geiger Road.

Chapter 11

LaSALLE TOWNSHIP
(OTTER CREEK)

Cousino

Cousino was located about two miles south of Lasalle off Cousino Road, just after Victory Road. It was a station for the Detroit & Toledo Shore Line Railroad. Interestingly enough, the railroad actually had a track specifically for loading sugar beets. Cousino also had the Muddy Creek School, located on Muddy Creek and Cousino Roads; it shows up on the 1859 Geil map. A second school was built after 1876, southwest of the first school. In 1948, it sustained tornado damage, and in 1949, it became part of the Custer School District. Today, the school is a private residence at 4709 North Muddy Creek Road.

On June 25, 1964, a train riding on the Detroit and Toledo Shore Line Railroad crashed at Cousino Road in LaSalle at one o'clock in the morning. The train was northbound to Detroit when the wheels suddenly left the track. Fifteen freight cars were hurled on top of each other in a huge, twisted-up mess. Giant rolls of steel, coal and sand were intermingled in a heaping, unrecognizable pile. The solid steel rails were bent into *S* curves. Miraculously, no one was injured. Damages were estimated to be around $110,000. No cause was ever determined.

Cousino shows up on a 1930 map and other maps up until 1967, under Erie Township.

Former Muddy Creek School today. *Author.*

Hall School District

Very little is known about Hall School District, other than that it shows up on a 1916 map and was mentioned in the *Monroe Evening News* on January 5, 1923. There was a Hall School at Dunlap and Stein Roads, but it is no longer there. Chances are a small area developed around the school, which tended to happen in these towns. They also developed around families' homes, churches, businesses and the like.

Toledo Beach

Toledo Beach Amusement Park was actually a resort town but also a station on the Toledo, Ottawa Beach and Northern Railroad. Around the state line, the railroad connected to the Detroit and Toledo Shore Line Railroad. Originally, the area was called the Ottawa Beach Resort, but it was bought out by the Toledo Rail Light and Power Company. The company built the resort in 1907 on the four-hundred-acre parcel, which

Above: Toledo Beach postcard. *Author.*

Left: Former interurban railroad bridge, Luna Pier. *Author.*

was only accessible by railroad, as the railroad had planned. The hamlet of Toledo Beach got its own post office on May 29, 1915, with Albert C. Van Driesen as the first postmaster.

The interurban line—the Toledo, Ottawa Beach and Northern Railway—was very popular, and it only took thirty minutes to get from downtown Toledo to the resort. The neighborhoods of Venice, Lakeside and Lakewood formed near the shoreline. To entice people to the area, the railroads offered attractions such as death-defying acrobats and high-flying diving artists. One of the highlights for the park was when Harry Atwood flew his Wright brothers plane over the resort in 1913. People were absolutely amazed. In 1911, Atwood was a student at the Wright brothers' school in Dayton.

In 1905, a grandiose dance hall with wooden floors was built that also served as a roller rink. Over the years, the park exploded, and by 1950 it offered many attractions, such as train rides and a large water slide. A Lake Chapel was even built. Toledo Beach existed until 1962, when it was sold and demolished to make room for the new Toledo Beach Marina.

Today, the only remnants of the once-popular resort are the tracks of the interurban line, the remains of the powerhouse at the Toledo Beach Marina and the bridge going across Whitewood Creek in Luna Pier at the public boat dock area. Toledo Beach shows up on a 1955 map.

WINCHESTER

Winchester was possibly named after General George Winchester, who directed the American troops at the Battles of the River Raisin. The settlement was located at the mouth of Otter Creek. It had a railroad station, a post office, a hotel, a general store, a church and a school.

The LaSalle Village School was located between North and South Otter Creek Roads and bisected by North Monroe Street. The school shows up on the 1859 Geil map at North Otter Creek Road and Dixie Highway. In 1872, a larger brick school replaced the old one; it ran until 1954 and was torn down a year later. Today, the property is the home of the Lasalle Fire Department.

The old Winchester post office is an apartment complex today. The door from the old post office, as well as a mail scale, can be seen in the current post office. Otherwise, nothing is left of the hamlet of Winchester.

Winchester first shows up on the 1859 Geil map and shows up on other maps up through 1930 or so under Lasalle Township.

Above: Former Winchester old post office. *Author.*

Left: Original Winchester post office door. *Author.*

Yargerville

Yargerville was a settlement named after (Richard) Robert Wells Yarger. Robert was the son of John and Margaret Yarger. He was born in Pennsylvania and came to the area in 1850. The hamlet was located at the intersection of East Morocco, Wood and Minx Roads, between the townships of Ida and Lasalle. Yarger opened a general store and ran a gristmill, a sawmill and a creamery. There was also a pump house and a blacksmith shop. Addison Barron ran a general store, as did Charles Scheurer. Scheurer had everything you could possibly need in his store but little to no meat, since there was no refrigeration back then.

Yargerville had a post office from 1890 to 1906; Yarger became the first postmaster on January 30, 1890. Yargerville School was built before 1859 and located on Strasburg Road. It was used until 1872, when it was replaced with a larger brick school, farther north and across the street from the first one. It had a thick stone foundation, a hardwood floor and thick brick walls. It was used until 1948 and eventually torn down.

Today, the only remnant of Yargerville is the road named after it. The village shows up on the 1896 Ogle map and up through 1972 on other maps under Samaria and Lambertville.

Chapter 12

LONDON TOWNSHIP

Blue Bush

Blue Bush was actually a town, not just a road as it today. It was established in the 1800s but had ceased to exist by 1910. Blue Bush had a Catholic church and a cemetery, both established in 1857. The church used to be located next to the cemetery at the intersection of Hoffman and Liedel Roads. The cemetery is still there and is St. Joseph's Cemetery today, run by Divine Grace Parish.

There was also the Gramlic School, which appears on the 1859 Geil map at the corner of Liedel and Hoffman Roads. It was rebuilt before 1876 just a little south of the first one. It was used until 1967 and still exists as a private residence at 9370 Hoffman Road.

In the 1830s, John and Abigail Critchett moved to the area, and the rumor was that they used their home as a safe house for slaves making their way to Canada.

Mary Haag came to the area with her parents in 1865, and they settled at Blue Bush on parcel no. 14, as shown on the 1876 Beers atlas (as "I.F. Haag"). She married Louie Knittle, and they settled in Azalia, where he became a blacksmith.

Genesco

In the 1800s, Genesco was plotted to be in the northeast quarter of section 19 in London Township in the Monroe County deed books. But according to the maps of the time, it does not appear that it ever came to fruition as planned. In the corner of section 19 was the Barnes School, at Plank and Allison Roads; it shows up on the 1859 Geil map. In 1876, it was rebuilt across the road, and in 1954, it was closed.

In section 20, just down the Plank Road between Townsend and Allison Roads, was a Congressional church and a Methodist church. Next to the church, on Plank Road, was a cemetery. Today, the church and the London Township Cemetery still exist.

Lisbon

Lisbon was established in 1837 on the Saline River in London Township. According to the 1859 Geil map and the 1876 Beers atlas, there was a school located by the Saline River, Fryburg School, at 13222 Plank Road. It was used until 1954, and today, it is a private residence. Also in this area—on the Saline River, right at the Milan border, in the northwest corner of the township—was a hotel, a cheese factory, a sawmill and a cider mill. This seems like the most probable location of Lisbon.

London

London was actually a settlement within the township located at Plank, London and Ostrander Roads. It got its own post office on December 22, 1832, and ran until February 15, 1905, with Henry Post as the first postmaster. There was a school, a couple general stores and a quarry. The London Sand Quarry was established at the intersection of Darling and Tuttle Hill Roads. The Ostrander-Palmer Schoolhouse was located on 9805 Townsend Road and is still there today as a private residence.

Many notable people settled in London. William Ostrander was born in New York in 1828 and came to London in 1856. He was a farmer, a merchant and a postmaster. He paid out of his own pocket to have the mail carried from Raisinville to London.

Right: Genesco
Methodist Church.
Milan Public Library.

Below: Fryburg
School today. *Author.*

Former Ostrander-Palmer Schoolhouse today. *Author.*

E.R. Palmer was born in London in 1840. Besides being a farmer, he dealt in stocks and served as a school inspector and drain commissioner in London.

Burton Snell was born in 1842; he was a farmer as well as a veterinary surgeon in London.

Robert Royal was born in England in 1844 and came to the United States in 1851; in 1871, he made his home in London. He practiced farming but was also a justice of the peace, a drain commissioner, a constable and a deputy sheriff for four years.

James A. Blackner was born in 1832 and came to London in 1870. In 1878, he bought up A.W. Hardy's merchandise business and opened his own store. In 1873, he was elected justice of the peace, and in 1879, he served as the postmaster.

John Pool was born in 1831, and in 1879, he settled in London as a farmer. For many years, he served as constable of the township, and in 1884, he was made deputy sheriff of Monroe County.

London shows up on the 1859 Geil map and up through 1967 on other maps, under Maybee. There is also mention of a "West London" in the January 11, 1922 *Monroe Evening News*.

Oakville (Readingville, Nelsonville)

Oakville was settled in 1831 and was so named because of all the oak trees in the area. Cyrus Everett, the first town supervisor, built the first home there in 1831. That same year, Asa H. Reading and David Hardy built a water-powered sawmill. A post office opened on May 7, 1834; Ichabod S. Nelson served as its first postmaster until it closed on November 24, 1834. It was restored in January 1935, with Nelson as postmaster again. But in May 1835, Asa H. Reading was named postmaster, and on May 2, 1835, he renamed the village Readingville. In June 1836, a year later, Nelson once again took over as postmaster, and he changed the name of the settlement to Nelsonville. Finally, on January 3, 1837, it was named Oakville. The post office closed on February 29, 1904.

The Oakville School was established in 1880 at Tuttle-Hill and Oakville-Waltz Roads. After 1901, it was rebuilt across the road and ran until 1954. The first school is a private residence today, at 14339 Tuttle Hill Road.

There was also a Methodist church and a general store in Oakville. In the 1920s, Eddie's Wayside Tavern was very popular; owned by Ed H. Sibolske, it offered dancing every weekend.

Oakville School, 1915. *Milan Public Library.*

Another notable resident was Harry Ross, who was born in 1828 and was a blacksmith in Oakville when he settled there in 1886.

Reuben M. Reynolds was born in 1829 and came to Oakville in 1856. One year later, he built a business for the manufacturing of barrels and a repair shop to fix wagons and carriages. Later, he patented a wagon jack, which procured him a fair amount of money.

Thomas C. Howard was born in 1848 and came to Oakville in 1880. He bought a general store, in which he sold a variety of items, such as dry goods, groceries, fish and produce. He also exported poultry and cattle to Detroit. He served as the supervisor of London twice and also as treasurer.

Nothing really exists of Oakville today. It shows up on the 1859 Geil map and is on other maps up through 1967 under Maybee.

Reighley (Raleighville)

Reighley was established in 1836, but apparently not much came of it but an idea on paper. There is a map of it in the Monroe County deed book.

A Raleighville Cemetery was established in 1876 at 13987 Townsend Road. Today, it also goes by the name of Pool-Townsend Cemetery. In the 1876 Beers atlas, it was on land owned by Jane Pool, parcel no. 9.

The Raleighville School was built before 1859 at 12099 Darling Road. In 1873, it was rebuilt out of bricks, and it stayed at the same location until it closed in 1951. Today, it is a private residence.

Chapter 13

MILAN TOWNSHIP (FARMERSVILLE, WOODARD MILLS, MOOREVILLE, TULANVILLE)

AZALIA (EAST MILAN)

Azalia was known as East Milan when it was founded. The Toledo, Ann Arbor and Grand Trunk Railroad opened a depot in Azalia on June 8, 1878. Then, in the summer of 1880, the Detroit, Butler and St. Louis Railroad opened a depot there. Azalia got its first post office on August 4, 1869, with Stephen B. Frink as the first postmaster. The post office was renamed Azalia after the first railroad depot opened in 1878. The name is rumored to have come from Azalia Ashley, daughter of a railroad tycoon.

In 1856, Shobel Lewis founded the Azalia Methodist Episcopal Church. A new brick building was built in 1870. The Azalia Cemetery next to the church is the resting place of some of the earliest families of Azalia. There was also a Christiancy Cemetery, which has long since deteriorated and is no longer recognizable as a cemetery. The Azalia School was built sometime after 1876 at the intersection of Crowe and Couper Roads; it consolidated with Milan Schools in 1955. Bisby Select School was also organized in Azalia in 1885.

Azalia was also called Reeves Corners, or Reeves Station, after Sayre (or Sayer) W. Reeves and his son, who opened up a woodworking factory called the Star Bending Factory. The factory focused on making wagon wheels and employed a number of men. It was located on Ostrander Road west of town. Later, it burned down in the big town fire of 1889—quite a

Azalia Church today. *Author.*

loss to the town. Sayre used to be a resident of Dexter, Michigan, and had quite the jaded past.

Sayre Reeves was born on November 19, 1807, in New York. He married Betsy Youngs in New York on January 13, 1830. She was born on June 14, 1807; died on July 6, 1878; and is buried in Azalia Cemetery with her husband. During their union, they had ten children. They came to Azalia around 1835.

Sayre and his family had a successful tavern in Dexter, then hit hard times. The destitute Sayre squatted on land that was actually a floodplain; due to the Peninsula Flour Mill's dam, it flooded every spring, leaving Sayre and his family to deal with the mess and illnesses this caused. He filed a lawsuit against Jesse and George Millerds, the mill owners, in 1843. A year later, he was awarded damages of $250. But the Millerds refused to give him a penny and filed an appeal, and the case dragged on in court for another year. So Sayre, his brother-in-law Jonas Young, James Jacobus and two others plotted to take matters into their own hands. On May 1, 1845, under the cover of darkness, they set out to destroy the wooden dam—and Sayre was determined to shoot anyone who got in their way.

But somehow, the farmers in the area got wind of the plan—and they were fit to be tied. The mill and, consequently, the dam were their lifeline; they depended on the mill to grind their wheat so they could sell it. So twenty of them amassed to stop Sayre. They surprised him and his group at midnight on May 2. Twenty-three-year-old Alfred Deforest Phelps, son of Isaiah and Clarissa Phelps, led the attack. In the melee, Sayre fired his weapon in the general area of the group, but the bullet struck Phelps. Phelps died on-site shortly thereafter. Sayre's immediate reaction was to flee, throwing his gun into the millrace.

The town was put on high alert, and by morning, Sayre and his fellow perpetrators had been caught by the townspeople and thrown in jail. At Sayre's first court appearance, tempers flared, and screaming filled the courtroom. On May 7, 1845, the *Michigan State Journal* published an article, "Disorder in the Courts," about the melee at the arraignment of Sayre Reeves. But Sayre and his cohorts served little time. Even though Sayre was accused of trespassing, destruction of property and murder, he was never "formally" charged with any of it. Ironically, in 1847, he lost his case in the appeals court for his $250 award from the mill owners, the Millerds, from 1844. By 1850, he had decided to take his large family and get out of Dodge, if you will; he ended up relocating to Oakville in London Township. Luckily for him, it seems his past did not follow him, and he was successful in running a stagecoach stop/hotel near Plank Road. He even opened up a sawmill in 1870.

Sometime before 1876, Sayre uprooted his family again and moved to Azalia, where he and his son William started the Star Bending Factory. Sayre ended up owning a lot of land in Azalia by the time he passed away on December 31, 1877. He was buried in the Azalia Cemetery.

The story takes an even more incredible turn when we look at who Sayre's offspring married. After the family moved to Oakville, teenager Mary Reeves moved back to Dexter. One day, while she was working in a store downtown, she met Charles T. Sill, and they married when Mary was twenty-two years old, in 1862. But surprisingly, Charles was the nephew of Deforest Phelps—the man Sayre shot in 1845. His mother, Deforest's sister, was Almira, and she was at the wedding of her son, when he married Sayre's daughter. The newlyweds kept the family secret to themselves, especially after they moved to Milan. They eventually built a home at 180 East Main Street. In 1900, William Reeves built a large Victorian home next to his sister's at 200 East Main Street. Still later, Charles's sister Alice Sill married Russell Reeves, Sayre's nephew. The Reeves family's efforts to leave the past behind were

Former William Reeves home, Milan. *Author.*

successful due to the day and age in which they lived. Today, of course, this would not even be close to possible.

Oddly enough, another story so unbelievable it sounds like a dramatized work of fiction came out of Azalia and the Sayre/Reeves family connection to a gentleman there by the name of Edward Ferrie Couper. Sayre and his son William employed Couper at the Star Bending Factory. Couper's story, however, would send shock waves throughout the community of Azalia, while Sayre's story remained hidden. Edward Ferrie Couper was born in England on January 15, 1859, to James and Marion (Miller) Couper. The family ultimately made their way to Azalia.

The problems started when Edward Couper crossed paths with the wife of Milton Waite. Milton Waite—who was born on December 24, 1849, to Wilder Waite and Ruth A. (Reem) Waite—fell in love with Azalia resident Diantha Smith, daughter of Henry O. Smith and Diantha (Jones) Smith. Diantha was born on February 18, 1855. Milton and Diantha were married in 1880 and had a daughter the same year. Milton was employed by the railroad. After just three years of marriage, problems arose when bachelor Edward Couper met and fell in love with Diantha. Rather than accept the circumstances, Couper took drastic action one night in 1883, climbing into the second-story window of the Waite's log home and proceeding to stab Waite in the leg with a knife. In the struggle, Waite managed to overpower Couper and throw him down the stairs. Couper fell to the floor, bleeding profusely—but he managed to escape and drag himself over a mile to his home. On the way, he ditched his rubber boots and the knife in a rain barrel behind a neighbor's house.

The story got stranger when Diantha unwittingly revealed her role in the crime. When she and Couper were questioned by the police, she told them that they had a plan: if Couper, after sneaking into the bedroom, grabbed the wrong leg, she would wiggle her toes to let him know that it was her and he needed to move to the other side of the bed. Although Couper's tracks were found going back to his house, the case was never prosecuted. No charges were filed by the Waites. Couper's father, James, told Diantha's father, Henry O. Smith, "If my son sings, your daughter sings too." After a while, the fiasco died down. Diantha was apparently content to stay Milton's wife and have another child with him in 1891. Milton Waite died on April 7, 1923, leaving Diantha a widow.

Diantha ended up marrying George Bunce at some point between 1923—when they both became widowers—and 1930. But sometime before 1937, Diantha was a widow again. She died on March 1, 1937. Couper eventually married Bertha Aiston in 1888, but she died in 1889. He married a second time to Jennie Elizabeth McArthur in 1897. He ended up having five children.

The Waites and the Coupers were all buried in the Azalia Cemetery. But that is not the end of the story: ironically enough, a road named after the Couper family in Azalia still exists today.

Gertrude Lafler remembered that when she was eight, after their house in Egypt burned, she and her parents moved into the Waiteses' house in Azalia. She said she could see where the blood still stained the wood floor in the Waiteses' bedroom.

Azalia became quite the boomtown, with plenty of industry and mercantile businesses. There were also plenty of lime kilns and stone quarries. The Nogar Stone Quarry was located by Bigelow and Bunce Roads. There was also a hotel for the quarry workers until about 1910. Just north of town, George and Henry Myers owned a sawmill; they also made bricks and tiles in large kilns there. Many "tramps" hung around there for warmth. At the northwest corner of Azalia and Ostrander Roads was a tile yard. There was another sawmill behind Carl Bruckner's house.

Successful businessman E.M. Lewis of Azalia opened a general store in 1877. But he was mostly known for his first charcoal kiln, which he built in 1881. He eventually had seven of them. On average, he consumed 4,000 cords of wood per year to produce 130,000 bushels of charcoal. Then, in 1884, he opened a brick and tile works. Two years later, in 1886, he had fourteen men working for him, and he produced 450,000 bricks and 250,000 tiles. On top of all this, he also had a portable sawmill and owned a two-hundred-acre farm.

Salesman Fred H. Noble from Toledo decided to hop off the train at Azalia one day with all his samples. He met W.C. Reeves, the owner of the general store, and ended up selling him $800–$900 worth of merchandise—a lot in those days. Then Reeves asked Noble if he knew anyone that would like to buy an interest in his store. It turned out that Fred Noble's son, William, was so interested that by nightfall he owned half the store and within six months owned the whole thing. He also became postmaster and settled in Azalia in 1894 at the corner of Ostrander and Azalia Roads.

The general store, now known as Noble's Store, lacked for nothing. It functioned as a post office, a clothing store, a shoe store and a drugstore, as well as selling groceries. In 1904, William Noble built a new brick store building next to the old one, complete with a second floor. The store had a dual purpose, as the second floor served as a social gathering place with its hardwood maple flooring, which was perfect for dances and other social activities. It became known as the Gleaners Lodge. One thing it did not have was liquor; Azalia never had a saloon or any liquor at all.

Joseph W. Meadows ran the grain elevator at Azalia for its owner, who lived in Ann Arbor. He also had a grocery store, and the post office was located there. When Noble bought Reeves's store, though, the post office was moved to Noble's Store. There existed a big rivalry between the two stores. But Meadows's store burned down in 1886.

The Civil War impacted Azalia just like it did every town. When it was finally over in 1865, about two dozen soldiers from Monroe County were anxious to get home. Azalia settler Myles Frink was one of them. Myles, the son of Stephen and Sally Frink, was in Company H of the Twelfth Michigan when he was captured at Athens, Georgia, charging the fort on September 24, 1864. He was thrown into a Confederate prison camp, and luckily for him, he survived the ordeal and could finally dream of getting back home.

On April 27, 1865, Myles boarded the 260-foot wooden steamboat *Sultana* at Memphis, Tennessee, headed for home. He was among 2,000 soldiers on a ship that was only supposed to carry 376. Overloaded and having suffered

Azalia Tile & Brick Factory, 1901. *Milan Public Library.*

Azalia railroad depot, 1908. *Milan Public Library.*

Top: Fred H. Noble store, Azalia, 1907. *Milan Public Library.*

Bottom: Former Fred H. Noble store today. *Author.*

from boiler problems just a few days earlier, the ship struggled against the strong current of the spring thaw, and the boilers burst, spewing flames into the air. The ship was done for. Out of 2,000 men, only 200 survived; 1,800 perished. The *Sultana* would forever be known as the "deadliest maritime disaster in U.S. history—worse than the *Titanic*," according to *Smithsonian Magazine*. Out of those from Monroe, 36 percent or so perished, including Myles Frink. Myles is buried in the Azalia Cemetery.

Blanche Davis, who was born in 1879, remembered that when she was a nine-year-old child, her grandfather Thaddeus Ball had a sawmill at Dundee-Azalia and Oelke Roads. But what she remembers most is when a family member came to visit her grandfather and Thaddeus got smallpox after the visit. Then Blanche's mother came down with it. Three other cases also broke out in Azalia. Thaddeus succumbed to the disease and was buried right away. When someone died from such a thing, they were to be buried hurriedly and in a secret place. No one wanted to do the burial for fear of catching the disease. Blanche said that the whole community was in a panic about the ailment.

While Blanche's mother was sick upstairs in bed, there was a knock on the door. A strange man was at the door and forced some papers into Blanche's hands, thus "serving papers" from the township declaring that their house was now considered a "pesthouse." No sooner than the man headed away than two men came up with a stretcher and dropped off Frank Reeves, who lived down the road and was suffering from smallpox. The house was chosen because the disease had already visited it. It was also a large house that could hold many diseased people and stood off on its own on ninety acres.

Patients were coming and going from midwinter until the spring of 1889, when the disease finally ran its course. Blanche thinks at the most, there were nine patients at a time. One was the local doctor, Dr. Randal Schuyler, who at one time had ninety smallpox scabs on his thumb. Dr. Schuyler graduated from the University of Michigan in 1877 and came to Azalia the same year to set up his practice. In 1886, he opened a pharmacy.

Dr. Mesick from Milan came to check up on the patients regularly, wearing a red handkerchief over his face for protection. Two medical students from the University of Michigan also came to help, as well as a cook. Blanche herself also helped do little things for the patients, like bringing them water. The patients who were recovering would gather in the living room at night around the stove and pick their scabs off with a penknife. Blanche was tasked with sweeping all the scabs up off the floor in the mornings. But she said that no one died of smallpox at their house, and Blanche herself never got sick. When the outbreak was finally over, everything in the house was burned except the wooden furniture and the house was fumigated.

Despite these precautions, everyone avoided the house after that, and Blanche said even the trains went faster when they passed by. Her mother was compensated $400–$600 for the use of the house. But it was of little help; with all the food gone and everything in the house having been burned, Blanche said that they were nearly destitute for many years.

The impact of the smallpox outbreak on Azalia cannot be overstated. It devasted the community. Schools closed for two weeks, and there were no church services for three weeks. On January 24, 1889, the *Ann Arbor Register* reported that the outbreak consisted of fourteen cases in Azalia and the town was

> *well guarded, and no one is allowed to leave except one or two whose business it is to provide necessities....Its 200 inhabitants are largely composed of railroad employees, lumbermen and charcoal burners. The epidemic and consequent quarantine has resulted seriously for them. They are mostly poor men, and with the stoppage of work has ceased their source of revenue.*

But as if that was not enough, the nail in the coffin came soon after. In the same year, 1889, six-year-old Emma Monk woke up one morning to an amazing sight—one that would change her life forever. She could barely believe her eyes when she saw, from her bedroom window, flames soaring high into the sky. At the time, she did not know it, but she was witnessing one of the largest, most destructive fires in the area's history. The fire was even raging across the creek in town, and "men were carrying pails of water from the little stream and pumps but weren't able to do much to stop the flames." Relentless winds wreaked havoc, fanning the flames to the stores at the corner of Ostrander and Dundee Roads. Emma recalled, "It looked as though the whole town might burn." Del Reynold's General Store and the Star Bending Factory were completely engulfed in flames. By the end of it, over two dozen buildings along Ostrander Road were destroyed.

Today, all that remains of Azalia is Azalia Road, as well as the Azalia church, the Azalia cemetery, some houses and a converted store building that used to be Noble's Store. Azalia shows up on the 1896 Ogle map and other maps up through 1967 under Milan.

Cone (West Milan)

Cone, originally known as West Milan, was basically bisected by the counties of Washtenaw and Monroe. In 1831, Erastus S. Cone moved with his wife, Nancy Thomas, from Vermont to Port Lawrence, Michigan. Erastus was born to John Cone and Rebecca Sage on December 11, 1798, in Westminster, Vermont. Erastus married Nancy on July 16, 1820. In 1833, he

Downtown Cone, 1907. *Milan Public Library.*

started buying land in West Milan. At some point, the family moved to West Milan, and within a year, Erastus and Nancy were divorced. On January 12, 1848, Erastus married Sarah Uptegraph, who was eighteen to Cone's fifty. Sarah became a stepmother to six kids, most of them older than her. In 1866, Erastus served as a justice of the peace. He eventually added eleven more children to the six he already had, for a total of seventeen. Ironically enough, the last child was born only six days before his father died at age seventy-one on April 14, 1869.

John Cornelius Cone, son of Erastus and Nancy, was born on February 19, 1827, and later moved to West Milan with his family. When the post office was put in on August 4, 1869, John became the first postmaster; he served until 1885. The post office ran until September 15, 1917. In 1880, the Wabash Western Railroad arrived and named its depot Cone after postmaster John, thus prompting the post office to change its name to Cone in 1881–82. John owned a lot of land in Cone and ran a stave business and a brick and tile company. He was married five times, becoming a widower each time. John died at seventy-two years old on November 1, 1899, and is buried in the Rice Cemetery.

In its heyday, about thousand families lived in Cone, although many resided in little shacks. There was a school, a couple churches, a grain elevator, a couple barrel factories, two stores, sawmills, charcoal and brick kilns, a sugar beet factory and even a medical office, run by Dr. George W. Richardson.

Cone depot, 1907. *Milan Public Library.*

Downtown Cone, 1907. *Milan Public Library.*

The Cone School was built at the intersection of Dennison and Cone Roads in the 1850s. After 1859, a new school was built next to the original one and ran until 1954, when it consolidated with Milan Schools.

In 1846, the Immaculate Conception Church was organized by Reverend Pierre Smothers of Detroit. It was attached to the parish in Ypsilanti. The church was constructed in 1848 and got an addition in 1855. The church was located on Welch Road, west of Dennison Road. Portions of the Peter Hanlon and William Johnston farms were used for the church and a cemetery. It was open through World War I, but after that, the church was moved and used as a granary, leaving the cemetery abandoned. In 1866, the Reverend Thomas Lupton (or Coupton) founded the Methodist Episcopal church, which held services in the old schoolhouse. A church was built in the summer of 1867 and became known as the Cone Church.

Lumber was an important commodity for Cone. The abundant hickory trees and other hardwoods in the area provided material for the lime and charcoal kilns. This is also the reason that Hickory Road exists today. A good portion of the charcoal was sent to Ann Arbor by wagon, two hundred to three hundred bushels at a time. A byproduct of the charcoal kilns was lye, which, after the railroad came through, was in high demand and was shipped out in wooden barrels on flatcars. Lye was used in making lye soap. Basswood trees were plentiful and used for twine. The outer layer of bark would be peeled back and the inner layer cut into strips. Sycamore trees in the area were used for smokehouses, as they were mostly hollow at the base; the settlers would cut a tiny door in the trunk and smoke their meat right inside.

The soil was rich for growing sugar beets, and Cone became a major supplier of sugar beets to a sugar company in Owosso. For a while, Cone was Michigan's sugar beet capital. Beets came in so fast from the farmers that the railroad cars could not haul them all and the plant in Owosso could not handle the large quantity coming in. So loads had to be weighed and then piled in long rows next to the railroad siding. There they could be stored in huge hoppers and dumped into railroad cars when they were ready for them.

There were two general stores in Cone, one owned by Frank Raymond and the other by a Mr. Auten. Both stores had dance halls on the second floor and held dances one or two times a month. People came from miles around to attend. For fifty cents' admission, people could enjoy dancing to live music by a three-piece band. They could also purchase dinner separately. There would be an average of 150 couples in attendance. Social life, especially in the winter, was pretty scant, so these dances were the highlight of the season. Before Prohibition, there was little interest in liquor in Cone, but Prohibition changed all that, with many farmers replacing their staple crops with crops needed to produce wine and beer, such as wheat, barley and hops.

The roads in Cone were like roads everywhere else at this time—a muddy mess. Once, while World War I was raging, there was a funeral in Cone. Cone resident Reverend Charles Bragg, who was to provide the service, left his house on Dennison Road at nine thirty in the morning for the two o'clock funeral at the Cone Methodist Church. On the way, he had to stop at a farmhouse and exchange his horse, who was exhausted from pulling a wagon with its wheels caked in heavy mud. After the service, the hearse, pulled by two horses, had to travel two and a half miles to the Rice Cemetery on Dennison Road. Bragg and the pallbearers decided to walk the Wabash Railroad tracks to the cemetery instead. They actually got there first.

The Rice Cemetery was named after farmer Josephus Rice, whose father, Caleb, purchased the land for him in 1833. The family lived in New York, and Josephus left to come farm the land in Cone at some point. He donated the land for the cemetery from some of the farmland. He married Mary Goss, and they had six children. One of them, Nelson Oliver Rice, born in 1846, served as Cone village assessor for five years and village councilman for a number of years. The Josephus Rice family is buried in the Rice Cemetery.

Electric Lights come to Cone, 1907. *Milan Public Library.*

An existing grain elevator in Cone was purchased in 1939 by J.B. Squires. Squires revitalized it, but in the 1950s, it barely survived a fire. Yet after that, Squires had eight 120-foot-tall silos built, which can still be seen today.

As in many of the other towns in this book, after the arrival of the automobile, Cone's kilns and mills were no longer necessary, the railroads stopped, abandoned stores burned down and the Cone church was sold. Today, little exists of the former community of Cone but the road bearing its name.

Cone shows up on an 1873 map and in the Beers 1876 atlas as West Milan; on other maps, it shows up to 1955 under Cone.

Chapter 14

MONROE CHARTER TOWNSHIP

(FRENCHTOWN)

FRENCHTOWN (MONROE)

The name Frenchtown has caused a lot of confusion because not only does the Township of Frenchtown exist, but the settlement of Frenchtown also once existed before becoming Monroe.

Like most of the United States, the area was first occupied by Native nations, mostly the Potawatomi. After the Revolutionary War, Great Britain ceded the lands northwest of the Ohio River, and the United States referred to these areas as the Northwest Territory, out of which Monroe was born. The Native nations utilized the rich soils and plentiful waters of the River Raisin and Lake Erie to sustain their settlements. They called the River Raisin the River of Sturgeon (Nummaseppe) because of all the sturgeon that made its waters their home. Many Native villages were spread throughout the area.

The first Europeans to settle in the region were primarily French Canadians. Many traveled south from Canada to Detroit. They first came to the area in the 1780s. The first settler is thought to have been Colonel Francis Navarre, who migrated from Detroit, as did most of the French Canadian settlers. They hoped to carve out their own niche in an area they heard had rich soil for farming; plenty of wildlife for sustenance and fur trading; and ample waterways and marshes teaming with fish. The French Canadians traded with the Native nations in Detroit and had a good relationship with them based on the fur trade commerce. In fact, Francis Navarre received a deed dated June 3, 1785, for his land from the Potawatomi.

The settlement soon saw an influx of French Canadians, who named it La Rivière aux Raisins due to the clusters of wild grapes hanging from the trees over the graceful waters of the river. They built their homes in the French style and within feet of the river, in proximity to each other. Even today, Monroe is unique because of its French layout; the French ribbon lot farms, which were unlike checkerboard grid patterns, can still be seen. The farms were called long ribbon lots due to the narrow but deep yards they had. In their lots, the settlers cultivated gardens and orchards. They usually marked their areas off with a puncheon fence (much like a picket fence). With all the French Canadians making the River Raisin their home, the area became known as Frenchtown. There were also a few settlers who were not French Canadian but Yankees, as the French called them.

The relationship between the Native Americans and the settlers was a cordial one, and thus the settlement grew rapidly, with intermarriage between the two groups. Before long, it was the largest métis (mixed) society in the territory. The area became so populated that, by the time of the War of 1812, homes extended up and down the river for twelve miles. It was the second-largest settlement in the territory, and it was thought it would soon rival Detroit. As more settlers poured into the area, especially non–French Canadians from the west and south, the demand for land grew as well. These land speculators did not wait for a treaty or deed to their land from the Native Americans but simply squatted where they desired. Tensions started to mount.

But everything changed with the Battles of the River Raisin during the War of 1812, fought in January 1813. The battles devasted the settlement. Many of the settlers fled the area, never to return. Those who did would fail to recognize the area they called home. And those who stayed faced the elements with little to no food, their homes and farms destroyed, their animals gone. The area was just a shadow of its former self. It would never regain its previous glory.

Years later, the area was reborn farther north following the River Raisin, as it had started to move north before the war. In 1817, the settlement was renamed Monroe after President James Monroe.

Above: Frenchtown ribbon lot farms. *Fran Maedel artist, River Raisin NBP.*

Opposite: Railroad remains in Greening. *Author.*

GREENING

Greening was an area two miles southeast of the city of Monroe that developed as a result of the Greening Nurseries. It all started in 1850, when German John Christoph Wilhelm Greening started the company on thirty acres in Monroe. In 1883, he was joined by his sons George A. and Charles C. Greening, and the business grew to over 1,500 acres. They promoted themselves as the "largest grower of trees in the world."

Greening got its own post office, but it only ran for five months, from March 3 to August 6, 1898, with Charles Greening as the postmaster. The hamlet was also an interlocked crossing of the Michigan Central Railroad and Detroit & Toledo Shore Line at First and Railroad Streets. The Michigan Central line actually had a spur directly into the Greening Nursery Company.

The Greening School was built in 1939 as a federal Works Progress Administration (WPA) project at 7385 East Dunbar Road. It was used for about ten years before it was closed. Today, it is a private residence. In 1921, the Greenings built a fancy office building out of "red velvet brick with white terra cotta" in downtown Monroe at 206 South Monroe Street; today, it houses Jack's Bicycle Shop. Workers' average wages were about 48 cents a day and the foreman's about $1.10 a day for working at the nursery.

In 1917, section foreman Frank Billings and three other Greenings employees sustained serious injuries when they were working on a handcar at the Greening railroad crossing. The four men were pushing the handcar along the tracks when, suddenly, a northbound Michigan Central train barreled into them from behind. The handcar flew off the tracks and hit foreman Billings in the process.

Greening shows up on a 1942 and a 1952 map under Monroe Township.

NEW DUBLIN

Irish workers employed on the River Raisin U.S. government canal in the 1830s settled together in an area on the southwest side of the city in the First Ward. It came to be known as New Dublin.

The New Dublin School ended up being one of Monroe's largest schools in the 1800s. It was located at the southeast corner of Harrison and Sixth Streets; it is no longer there. As it turns out, George Armstrong Custer went to school there. In 1849, at ten years of age, he came to Monroe from his home in New Rumley, Ohio, and lived with his half sister Lydia Reed. He attended the New Dublin school for a total of two years.

WARNER

Located about a mile north of the city of Monroe, Warner was a station for the Lakeshore and Michigan Southern Railroad established in 1882. The Warner yard, Michigan Central's main yard in the city, was along Michigan Avenue. The double main track splits at the yard, and there is an unusual loop track with a long crossover, allowing trains to maneuver in both directions. Today, the Warner yard is the Norfolk Southern yard at 601 North Dixie Highway.

Something odd kept occurring at the Warner yard: suddenly, burning gondola cars were seen heading there on multiple occasions in the 1960s. The fire department had to be called numerous times to douse them. After it happened twice in just a couple days, the mayor of Monroe and the fire chief contacted railroad officials about the problem. It appeared factories downriver were pouring hot refuse—fill for the Port of Monroe—into the cars, and the contents were catching fire on their way to Monroe. The problem was costing the city a lot of money at one hundred dollars an hour to douse the flames, not to mention the hazards of the pollutants in the air for the residents.

Warner shows up on a 1911 and a 1930 map.

Waterloo

Waterloo was a small area located in the First Ward of the city of Monroe, where today's Frenchmen's Bend subdivision is on North Custer Road. In 1820, a gristmill was built in this area on the River Raisin to produce flour by Miller and Jermain. In fact, the Waterloo Mills gained a reputation for its top-of-the-line flour and was the first mill to ship flour out of Michigan.

Waterloo Mills. *Monroe County Library System, Ellis.*

Monroe City Mills. *Monroe County Library System, Ellis.*

The contract was for two hundred barrels in 1927, destined to go east to New York.

A historical marker in the area states: "Waterloo Dam, title to which was acquired to unite park lands on the two banks of the river, marks the site of one of Michigan's earliest water power projects. The Waterloo Grist Mills… were established on the south bank of the river in 1820. The dam originally made of logs and heavy planking was re-built and concreted in 1904."

In 1836, the Monroe City Mills were founded by Judge Daniel Bacon, Ephram Frost and John Burch. They went into operation across the river from and kitty-corner to the Waterloo mills. A hydroelectric dam was built to sustain both mills. Frederick Waldorf bought both of the Monroe City Mills, which became known as the Waldorf Mill. Then, in 1895, the Amendt Milling Company purchased them. Up to this point, the mills were still operating by waterpower, but all that changed when a new roller mill technology was put in place. The mills became famous for their Lotus Flour.

The mills burned down in the horrific fire of 1890 when over half a mile of city businesses burned. It all started with just a spark from a railroad engine by the icehouse. The fire department used the River Raisin to their advantage fighting the Waldorf Mill fire and put their hand pumper right down into the river. Andrew Fragner was injured fighting the fire when a chimney collapsed and a brick fractured his skull. Dr. Lipke ended up removing a piece of Andrew's skull that was the size of a quarter. The family kept it in a button box and often retold the story. The doctor's instructions for recovery were, "Keep him covered up and make him sweat. Tie him down to his bed if you have trouble keeping him in it." Back then, doctors thought sweating it out was a good way for someone to heal. In any case, Andrew did indeed recover.

In 1852, Waldorf bought the Waterloo mills, then sold them to Norman and Perkins in 1858. Ownership changed again in 1870, when Stiles and Harvey entered the picture. The back-and-forth ownership of the mills went on for years. Sometime before 1908, the Waterloo mills also got in on the new roller technology, becoming known as the Waterloo Roller Mills. They produced the Gilt Edge brand of flour, which was very popular and well known. In addition to regular wheat flour, they also produced a fine buckwheat flour and cornmeal.

There was also a Waterloo sawmill, although the date it was established is uncertain. It would have been before 1834, because after John Chase came to Monroe in 1834, he worked in the Waterloo sawmill until 1840, when he started his own mill. Then, in 1850, he bought part of the Brookmer Mill in Raisinville and within a year bought it out.

Yet another mill was established at Waterloo by Thomas and John Norman soon after the gristmill was founded, but this was a woolen mill. It was located adjacent to the gristmill. The woolen mill produced wool fabric—like flannel—yarn and blankets. Over time, it passed through the ownership of Henry Shaw Noble, Herman J. Redfield and Plewes. Plewes invented an all-wool bed comforter that was made with treated wool batt. Edward G. and J. Lauer, along with Captain I.S. Harrington, purchased the mill in 1912 and kept Plewes on as supervisor.

There was a Waterloo School on the corner of Front Street and Telegraph Road. Before 1876, it was rebuilt on Front Street, a little way west of the first school. It was replaced yet a third time in 1927 and used until 1977, when it was torn down. Today's Waterloo School is in the same location. There was also the Waterloo farm, which was composed of two hundred acres and was bought up by Israel Epley Ilgenfritz in 1856 to grow plants for his nursery. The I.E. Ilgenfritz & Sons nursery (as it was later known) was a huge staple in Monroe and part of the reason it became known as the Floral City.

The Waterloo farm became the center of attention in 1839, when Deputy Sheriff James Mulhollen was in hot pursuit of a counterfeiter who escaped from jail. Mulhollen chased him all the way to the Waterloo farm, and when he finally caught him, they ended up in a brutal fight where the convict sliced off all the buttons on Mulhollen's vest. Mulhollen had no choice but to kill him in self-defense.

A very interesting resident of Waterloo was Seba Murphy, who was born in Rhode Island on July 25, 1787. When the War of 1812 broke out, he found himself stuck behind enemy lines in Canada. When he tried to cross the ice from Bath to get back to the United States, he got caught in a terrific snowstorm and found himself hopelessly lost. To top it off, he fell through the ice, and both of his feet sustained frostbite. He was found by a British picket guard and taken back as a POW to Canada. While there, he was treated, and both his feet were amputated. Murphy was not forgotten and later escaped by hiding under some bags of oats in the bottom of a sleigh. When he finally made it back to the United States, he settled in New York in 1818. In 1835, he moved to the city of Monroe. He ended up being a state senator, county commissioner, county treasurer and register of deeds. His home was at Waterloo Mills. He passed away on November 16, 1854.

Waterloo shows up on the Monroe city maps from 1900 to 1967.

Chapter 15

RAISINVILLE TOWNSHIP

EAST RAISINVILLE

East Raisinville was a hamlet in the township of Raisinville that grew up along the Lake Shore and Michigan Southern Railway. Samuel Atkinson was the founder and first postmaster of the Atkinson Post Office, established on May 22, 1829. The post office was originally named Atkinson after him, but its name was changed to East Raisinville on January 20, 1838. It ran until November 24, 1868.

Samuel, along with his wife, Mary, and son Lacey Amasa, who was eight years old at the time, settled in the area in 1827.

Darius Loose, born in 1821, also settled in East Raisinville and helped establish the Evangelical church there in 1863. He was also the superintendent of the Sabbath School for many years.

GRAPE

The village of Grape was founded in northwestern Monroe County along the River Raisin. It was named after the wild grapes growing along the River Raisin, technically by the son of David E. Morris, Joseph Wilson Morris. Joseph petitioned Washington, D.C., to name the village Grape. His father, David, originally settled in Grape on March 4, 1846, in the area by the Monroe-Milan Plank Road or the Monroe-Tecumseh Plank Road (North

Custer Road today). The plank road was a major throughfare at the time, laid out in 1827–29 by Anthony McKey and Nathan Hubble. The term *plank road* describes the way the road was constructed: of wooden planks, usually four inches thick by one foot wide. The planks were made in local sawmills and laid down side by side. In the spring, they would sink into the mud, making the road almost impassable at times.

After 1872, there were toll gates about every ten miles; the cost was set at two cents a mile but could be as much as three cents, depending on the number of axles. The family that lived nearest the gate collected the toll. About a mile outside of the village, the road split, with one branch going toward Milan and the other toward Dundee. Right at the split was the Plank Hotel. The tollkeeper and his family lived in the Plank Hotel, which was about twenty feet by twenty-five feet. By 1899, the hotel was in deplorable shape. Another hotel called the Junction Inn, or Pettit's Inn, at Plank and Bigelow Roads was popular in the 1830s.

German immigrant Peter Seitz arrived in Grape in 1850 and built the popular Seitz Tavern and Stagecoach Inn in 1856 on North Custer Road. The second floor was a ballroom, where numerous social events were held. In 1878, Peter died, and Louis Younglove bought the inn. Later, William Cominess bought it and converted it into his home in 1899; he lived there until 1965. (There is a historical marker on the side of the house, now a private residence at 8941 North Custer Road.)

In 1828, a wooden bridge over the river was constructed at Grape, at what today is Ida-Maybee Road. It was replaced at some point and lasted until 1888, when the citizens of Grape voted to build a steel bridge; it lasted until 1958, when a concrete one was put in. There was also a wooden bridge at the end of Doty Road. Back then, Doty Road ran straight through to the river; today, it stops at North Custer Road.

Joseph Doty and his wife, Sallie G. (True), left New York to settle in Raisinville Township and what would become Grape in 1839. They built their homestead and established their farm on forty acres next to the River Raisin. Originally, the town grew up in the area of the Doty homestead at North Custer and Doty Roads (their namesake), but later it shifted west. The mail was brought to the Doty farm for dissemination to the community. What would come to be known as the nondenominational old white church was built to the left of the Doty house in 1849. The first cemetery in Grape was the Doty Cemetery, established in 1841. When a neighbor passed away and there was no designated place to bury her, the family ended up donating a half-acre parcel to the right of the farm for the cemetery. It ended

Grape postcard. *Monroe County Library System, Ellis.*

up becoming a community cemetery, and each family took care of their loved ones' plots. There was no cost for a grave there. The homestead and cemetery still exist; access to the cemetery is via a long lane that runs parallel to the old farmstead at 6877 North Custer Road.

Resident Scott Brightbill was the first pony express rider for Grape and took care of delivering the mail to the Doty farm. He walked to and from Monroe on foot. He lived in what was known as the Stone Jug House and, for a while, distributed mail from there. He also built a gristmill and operated a quarry at Grape. He never married and lived until eighty years old. One day, in 1940, he was outside tending his garden next to the quarry, when he suddenly suffered a heart attack and fell into the quarry, which was filled with water at the time. He was later found deceased.

Former Peter Seitz tavern today. *Author.*

Former Joseph Doty homestead today. *Author.*

Former Stone Jug House today. *Author.*

The oldest structure in Grape today is undoubtedly the Stone Jug House. It sits at the end of Baldwin Road on North Custer. The house was constructed of limestone, which has yellowed with age. It was called the Stone Jug House because Baldwin Road used to be called the Stone Jug Road. The actual age of the house is debated. Some accounts say it was built in 1835. Others believe that it was built by Christopher Bruckner, whose deed says May 10, 1859. Bruckner owned the stone quarry. The original tract of land, before the house was built, was 240 acres, recorded in 1811. In 1855, the house was owned by Rachel Knaggs, but all the way up to 1942, it had up to 108 landowners, partly because of land split-offs. The house can still be seen today at the corner of Baldwin and North Custer Roads.

The various postal histories of Grape are contradictory. In many of these early towns, the post office was run out of a store, and the owner of the store was the postmaster. Sometimes the post office was run out of a house. In Grape, we have a couple houses listed as postal distribution areas: the Doty farm and the Stone Jug House. But multiple stores and different time periods are noted in other sources as well. Some of the stores from which mail was distributed are not known. One thing that seems certain are the official

RFD (rural mail route) No. 2, U.S. Mail. *Monroe Publishing Company.*

postal office records, which say a post office opened on June 1, 1887, and ran until October 15, 1906, with Hannah W. Atkinson as the first postmistress. But we shall see that even this is not quite correct. Although the location of this post office is uncertain, it is believed to have been run out of the store at the northeast corner of Doty and North Custer Roads. There is a mistake in the name, however, in the official post record; it should be Hannah B. Atkinson, not W.

We must revisit East Raisinville and Samuel Atkinson for a moment. You may remember that he was the founder and first postmaster of the Atkinson Post Office, established on May 22, 1829. The post office was originally named Atkinson after him, but its name was changed to East Raisinville on January 20, 1838. Samuel, along with his wife, Mary, and son Lacey Amasa, who was eight years old at the time, settled in Grape in 1827. Lacey Amasa Atkinson married Hannah B. Janney in 1849, and they established the Atkinson Farm at some point before 1859 (as it is parcel no. 472 on the 1859 Geil map). They ended up having five children. Hannah B. Atkinson followed in her father-in-law's footsteps and became the first female postmistress of the Grape Post Office. Although the post office is officially recorded as being put in on June 1, 1887, it was actually already there—as we can see if we look at the 1859 Geil map. It was located on parcel no. 495, owned by I.R. Grosvernor, but called the North Raisinville Post Office. The 1876 Beers atlas shows it in the same place, on parcel no. 495, as Grape Post Office, now on John Roessler's property (read on for more about him). According to the 1901 Lang map, Roessler apparently sold off some of his land by the river, because now the post office was located on property belonging to William Seitz Jr. (son of Peter Seitz; read on to learn about him). In any case, Hannah served as postmistress from June 1, 1887, to October 15, 1906. Unfortunately, some documents refer to her as Hannah W.—but her middle initial was actually B, as we have established.

The 1859 Geil map shows an A. Atkinson on parcel no. 472 (many other Atkinsons owned property as well), so Lacey Amasa (who went by the name Amasa) and Hannah Atkinson built their farmhouse in Grape before 1859. Rumor has it they also used their home as a station for hiding fleeing slaves on the Underground Railroad. Amasa never nailed down one of the steps leading up to the attic, which created a small but effective hiding place. The home was torn down in 1916. The white church built in 1849 on the Doty farm is thought to have a connection to Atkinson and the Underground Railroad as well, since it was located straight across the river from the Atkinsons' farm.

Grape was quite the boomtown in the 1860s: it had a few general stores, one of which included the post office, a grocery store, a hotel, several taverns, a cheese mill, a couple sawmills, a gristmill, a wagon factory, a cooper shop, a blacksmith shop, twenty lime kilns and several quarries. There were also a few churches, a couple cemeteries and two schools.

Former Bridge School, built 1828. *Author.*

Grape actually had the very first public school in Michigan; the original log one-room schoolhouse underwent construction on April 17, 1828, at 96 Ida-Maybee Road and was named the Barnaby School after the nearby Barnaby Farm. Later, it became known as Bridge School. In 1830, it was rebuilt larger. In 1868, a new brick version was constructed. In 1910, an addition was put on the building, and in 1928, the centennial stone tower was dedicated. The school closed in 1946. In 1960, the building received a historical marker for being Michigan's first public school, and it is a Michigan State Historic Site. Today, it serves the Raisinville Township Hall.

Grape resident William Cominess attended the Bridge School and had an unusual way to get to school. His father would row him in a rowboat across the river. The boys were required to haul wood after recess and at the end of the two sessions of the day to keep the wood-burning stove going. There was no well at the school, so the boys had to haul water from a nearby farm—which was not nearby, but eighty rods (a rod equals 16.5 feet) to the east. Everyone shared one pail of water and one drinking cup.

The village's second school, Grape School, shows up on the 1859 Geil map as south of North Custer Road and east of Doty Road on George Younglove's property. George Younglove settled in Grape around 1831. But evidently the school was rebuilt sometime before 1876, because in the 1876 Beers atlas, it is at a different location: on H.W. Moses's property. Later it became known as Raisinville School and ran until 1955; the building was torn down around 1965.

There were a few different churches in Grape, one at the corner of Doty Road—the old white church, which was previously mentioned. St. Matthew's Lutheran Church was built in 1879 on Ida-Maybee Road and is still there today, serving a different denomination. The Rath Cemetery was put in next to the church and also still exists today. Barnaby Methodist Church was located on Dixon Road on the Barnabys' property, kitty-corner from the Bridge School. The church was built around 1880 and used until the late 1920s; today, it is a private residence.

Various local industries brought in many workers as well as patrons. But mostly, Grape became synonymous with limestone. The sedimentary rock was all over the area by the river. It was utilized for building foundations. Many residents owned their own quarries. In a three-mile span, there were twenty lime kilns and numerous quarries. Heated limestone made a powdery mix and was used for mortar for brick and stone buildings, as well as plaster for interior walls.

Grape School. *Monroe Publishing Company.*

It is believed that the first kilns were built in 1840 by Christopher Bruckner, but there is some doubt; in any case, many farmers were in the lime business. In 1866, farmers Jake Seitz and Henry Rauch both operated lime kilns and quarries. Silas King owned lime kilns on both sides of North Custer, and Sid Younglove also operated a kiln. In the 1870s, Rauch put in a patent kiln instead of the pot kind everyone used. Pot kilns only held three hundred bushels, whereas the patent ones had three-foot thick walls with an inner box area of eight feet square.

William Cominess, born in Grape, remembered the details of the lime kiln business. The rock from the quarries was cut into squares and thrown into the kilns in pieces. Each pot kiln produced about three hundred bushels of lime. The lime would take up to three days to cook, and the fires had to be kept burning the whole time. Employees were paid from seventy-five cents to a dollar a day. Up to fifty men and twenty horses were needed to run the quarries, too. Cominess said it was common to have piles of wood waiting for consumption by the kilns, sometimes up to five cords. It was great business for the farmers, who could not keep up with the demand. Competition was keen, and feuds were common between farmers. Lime was usually twelve cents a bushel, but prices varied because of the competition. People came from miles away to Grape. Much of the lime produced in Grape went to Ypsilanti, Saline and Ann Arbor. Barrels were made, by Henry Miller, in the cooper shop to transport it. Cominess recalled, "As a boy I remember seeing teams and wagons lined up, awaiting their turn to load with lime. One poor fellow had come a long distance after a load and he became impatient while waiting for the lime to cool, so [he] started loading and his wagon caught on fire."

All in all, the kilns operated from the mid-1800s to 1905; the business's heyday was the around the turn of the century. But in 1905, everything changed when cement took over the limestone market. The last lime kiln in Grape was torn down in the 1920s.

In 1840, John Roessler was born in Germany, and he came to Raisinville Township with his parents in 1848. In 1862, he built a wooden dam across the river at Grape with wooden gates and bulkheads made of cement. The water at the dam was about sixteen feet deep and ran about eighty miles per hour. Roessler dug a millrace and built the Raisinville Flour and Feed Mills. Later, he built a sawmill, on the opposite side of the gristmills. Some sources say this sawmill was originally located west of the bridge and moved east to this location in 1862. In either case, it was an unusual one that utilized an upright saw, and consequently, the river would be jammed up with logs for miles on end due to farmers upstream cutting logs and then floating them to the mill. In one summer, the mill sawed five thousand feet of logs. Ultimately, there were two sawmills at Grape, but both declined after 1895, partly because of a lack of wood. The gristmill utilized five grindstones and produced feed, wheat flour and buckwheat flour. The mills had an unusual "umbrella wheel" in the basement area that went around horizontally. Roessler built his house directly in front of the mills on the south side of North Custer Road.

Dam at Grape. *Monroe County Library System, Ellis.*

Raisinville Flour and Feed Mills. *Marian Sisung.*

The farmers in Grape got together and decided there needed to be a cheese factory in Grape as well. George Knaggs had the land and relatives in New York familiar with running such a factory, so they invited them to come west to Grape. Ben William built the factory just north of the Grape bridge. New Yorker D.A. Jenkins also came to help run it. For many years, the farmers sold their milk to the factory for fifty cents per one hundred pounds. The cheese was cooked in two large metal vats that held about one hundred gallons each. It had to be stirred continually to achieve the desired consistency. Since the boiler had to be kept hot, someone had to feed it wood continually, too. The cheddar from Grape gained a reputation as a fine cheese sold under the brand Genuine Holstein Cheese for six cents a pound. The factory ran from 1895 to 1915, but it could not keep up with the larger factories in Detroit, which, during World War I, offered the farmers much higher prices for their milk. The factory was converted into a private residence for a while, then caught fire in 1966 and was destroyed.

By 1912, the Raisinville Flour and Feed mills were no longer turning a profit, and in 1915, Amendt Mill Company bought out the race and the gristmills and started generating electric power in Grape. The village was one of the first places in the county to get electric lights. The River Raisin Hydro-Electric Company served Maybee, Ida, Carleton and Scofield. But Amendt dictated to families when they were actually able to use the power, and they had designated wash and iron days. If there was low water, there was no power at all. No one was upset when Amendt finally sold out to Detroit Edison in the late 1920s. All traces of the mills are gone, as they were ultimately destroyed in 1946 with three charges of dynamite.

In 1918, the wooden dam was replaced with a cement one. The south bank, owned by George Rath Sr., was converted into Rath Park. It was popular in the 1920s to '30s. Admission was twenty-five cents a car. Incidentally, on January 9, 1997, the worst aviation accident to hit Monroe County happened on this piece of land. Comair Flight 3272, a twin-engine commuter plane traveling from Cincinnati, Ohio, to Detroit, Michigan, was flying through a snowstorm when the plane appeared to nosedive into the ground. All twenty-nine souls aboard were killed in the crash. The crash was later determined to have been caused by ice accumulating on the plane's wings.

William Seitz Jr., born in 1872 to Peter and Katherine Seitz, built a brick general store on the north side of road on what used to be John Roessler's property in 1902. The store also had a dance hall on the second floor. William ran a lime kiln, a sawmill, a cider mill and a cheese factory. John Seitz, his brother, built a hardware store across the street and was also a blacksmith.

Sidney Younglove store, Grape. *Monroe Publishing Company.*

His brother Henry Seitz ran a saloon and made sorghum. Henry bought the former store from Sidney E. Younglove. Sidney came to Grape in 1866 and in 1894 built his general store. He also ran a post office in the store in 1895 when he was postmaster. In 1899, he sold the store to Henry and left for Monroe, where he opened a harness shop. Then, in 1901, he opened a glove factory. Henry turned the store into a saloon.

Later, Henry's saloon was bought by John Gold, but Prohibition forced Gold to turn it back into a store. After Prohibition, Gold turned it back into a saloon and hotel. His hotel had only four rooms available and was often fully booked. People employed at Grape's cheese mill or lime quarries stayed there indefinitely. They were given a bargain at seven dollars per week, which included their room, laundry service and ironing. Gold ran the saloon until his death in 1940. Since then, it has operated as the Grape Pantry, with various owners. In the 1960s, the upper part of the building burned down, leaving only the first floor, which can be seen as part of the defunct Grape Pantry today.

Shortly after the turn of the twentieth century, William Seitz left Grape to go to Detroit with his brothers, John and Henry, to continue developing

Former Sidney Younglove store today. *Author.*

a truck William built as an experiment to see how a threshing machine ran. He was hoping to replace horses with a truck for hauling lime since he seen how much the animals suffered. It took six months to build the first Seitz Automotive and Transmission Company prototype truck at a cost of $3,500. Even though it only weighed three and a half tons, it could haul up to five and a half tons.

Ironically, many think it was the automotive that killed Grape. Oddly enough, Grape is associated with Henry Ford too. In 1885, twenty-two-year-old Ford was a mechanic for a company out of Port Huron, and he came all the way to Dixon Road in Grape to help out twenty-six-year-old farmer Christopher Rath with his broken-down threshing machine. History repeated itself in October 1927 when Henry Ford once more came to Grape to visit his now friend Christopher Rath. Ford picked up Rath in his Lincoln, took him to Greenfield Village for the day and even took him in an airplane ride over Detroit.

Without, question Grape was one of the largest lost towns in Monroe County. It enjoyed a long, prosperous industrial and merchant past. Surprisingly, there is nothing left to reveal its former glory. A few very old houses, the Stone Jug House, the Doty farmhouse, the Millers' house and a few others still dot the countryside. The bridge, school, cemetery, town hall, grange and church still exist in one form or another. A few of the old store buildings, huddled together in silence now, can still be seen on North Custer Road. Grape's mark on the landscape is perceptible to those who know some

Henry Ford (*left*) and Christopher Rath, Grape, 1927. *Monroe Publishing Company.*

Waterwheel, Grape. *Author.*

of the history—such as the quarries, now lakes on each side of the road. The remains of the millrace, the dam and the bulkhead peak over the overgrown cattails and reeds by the river.

A silent old sentinel sits among the weeds, an unbelievable survivor to attest to the once-hopping industrial center, now a rotted, twisted remnant of the age of the mill: a water wheel, no longer heard and barely seen as the land works to cover the scars on its facade. Can you hear the whispers of the past?

Grape appears on the 1859 Geil map as North Raisinville, then on other maps up to 1972 under Raisinville and Ida.

Hamlin (Raisinville Station, Brundleville)

Hamlin was named for Vice President Hannibal Hamlin, who served from 1861 to 1865. The village was a railroad station at the corner of Stewart and Yensch Roads. It got a post office on March 28, 1862, which ran until October 2, 1876. Calvin Clark was the first postmaster. The post office was transferred to Raisinville on October 2, 1876, and ultimately closed on October 15, 1906.

William Brundle ran a general store and the depot, but in 1929, they both burned down. Before this, Brundle also ran the Seitz general store in Grape.

This area appears on an 1873 map and on other maps up through 1909.

Raisinville/West Raisinville

Raisinville was established as a township, but there was a settlement of the same name. It was also called West Raisinville and Raisin. All these names are reminiscent of the name River Raisin. The settlement was located about four miles west of Monroe. In June 1825, it got its post office, which closed on March 20, 1828. Thomas B. Benjamin was the first postmaster. On November 28, 1832, the post office reopened under the name West Raisinville, yet its name was changed back to Raisinville on July 24, 1833. As if that was not enough, it was changed yet again to West Raisinville on January 20, 1838. It finally closed on February 17, 1842.

In 1898, the Raisin station became a stop on the Flint & Pere Marquette Railroad.

Colonel John Anderson was one of the first to settle the area in 1822, and in 1823, he sold his land to a Mr. Blanchard, who proceeded to clear the land and build a house. Only a few years later, Blanchard had to have his leg amputated. He became known for this incident, mostly because of his demeanor. It is said that he was very nonchalant about it—tossing his leg onto the table—and during the amputation he was observed only twitching a couple muscles as the surgeon reached the bone.

Other notable residents included Richard Peters, who was born in 1824 and served as superintendent of the town of Raisinville for about ten years while simultaneously farming.

Philip Titus was born in 1804 and came to Raisinville in 1845; he was a farmer and a blacksmith. In 1850, he built a tavern on his farm and was made gatekeeper of the Monroe Plank Road Company.

John Chase was born in 1817; in 1834, he came to Monroe and worked in the Waterloo Sawmill until 1840, when he started his own mill. Then, in 1850, he bought part of the Brookmer Mill in Raisinville and within a year bought it out.

The first paper mill in Michigan, called the River Raisin Paper Company, was established in 1838 in Raisinville at the junction of Raisinville and North Custer Roads. Christopher McDowell built the mill on the south side of the River Raisin. He used a unique system that all started in a small shack, where McDowell built a machine about thirty feet long by thirty-eight inches wide in which to dry paper. It was the first steam dryer west of the Alleghenies. The paper was wrapped around a ten-foot-diameter drum

Former Papermill School. *Author.*

while it was being dried by a fire. It produced a fine "rag" paper, which was used to print newspapers. The local newspaper, the *Monroe Gazette*, started using it in January 1839.

Mid-century, McDowell produced a butcher's paper made from straw. When he had his product ready, he pedaled it around in carts to the local merchants.

McDowell built his farm on the opposite side of the river, and later, he ended up putting in cottages for the mill workers south of the mill. A wooden bridge was constructed to cross the river around 1849.

The mill ended up having several different owners and finally closed in 1887. Other companies took McDowell's lead and built mills too.

In the 1850s, a school was built for the children of the paper mill workers and others in the area called the Papermill School. In 1887, the students had to row across the river to get to school when an ice jam floated the bridge away. It would not be replaced for eighty years. The Papermill School became part of the Monroe public school system in 1955 and ran until 1962. Today, it is part of the Monroe County Museum System and is interpreted as an old country store.

Norman J. Hall resided in Raisinville Township and attended the Papermill School. At the age of seventeen, he enrolled at West Point. He was the only soldier from Michigan at Fort Sumter when the Confederates bombarded it on April 12, 1861. This incident was considered the official start of the Civil War. On the second day of the attack, he noticed a shell had knocked down the flagpole, leaving the flag dangling. He would not stand for that and dashed through the shot and shell reigning down all around him to rescue the Stars and Stripes. He managed to grab the flag and run back to the fort, only to discover his hands, hair and even his eyebrows were singed. "The epaulets of his uniform had to be removed because they were so hot." Yet that did not stop him; despite his injuries, with a little help, he managed to create a new flagpole and once more raised the flag high.

In July 1862, Hall was put in charge of the Seventh Michigan Volunteer Infantry. They fought at Antietam, Fredericksburg and Gettysburg. At Fredericksburg, it was his brigade that that crossed the Rappahannock River in pontoon boats under a hail of gunfire in a mission to reach the city on the other side and clear out the Confederate sharpshooters. The action earned the Seventh Michigan its nickname, the Forlorn Hope.

The following year, the Seventh Michigan was at Gettysburg. They helped hold the Union line during Pickett's Charge at the Angle. Shortly after Gettysburg, in 1864, Hall had to go on disability because of typhoid fever he had contracted previously at Fort Sumter. He ended up dying of typhoid in Monroe at only thirty years old.

Today the only remnant of the Raisinville area is the Papermill School. The area shows up on the 1859 Geil map, then on other maps of Monroe County up through 1909.

South Raisin

An article in the March 15, 1923 *Monroe Evening News* mentions a Vandercook family living in South Raisin. Otherwise, nothing is known about this area.

Strasburg (Strasburgh)

In 1828, W.H. Rauch built the first lime kilns in this area, and the village of Strasburg ended up developing around that industry. A post office went in on June 24, 1874, with Eli Hausbarger as the first postmaster. It closed on July 11, 1876, but reopened on February 12, 1879, because the Lake Shore & Michigan Southern Railroad put a line through the village in 1878. After the railroad tracks to Adrian were built, August Braunlich of Ida nicknamed a corner of the train stop Strasburg, after Strasburg, France. It was actually a joke, since the only thing there was a few farmhouses. But the railroad helped grow the community, as most railroads do. The tracks were sandwiched between Dunbar and Albain Roads, with all the development occurring between the two. Back then, in the wintertime, the only way to Monroe was by railroad; there were no roads yet. It cost ten cents round trip. Demand was so high that a railroad ticket booth had to be built to keep up with all the sales.

Strasburg was quite the boomtown, with two general stores, a sorghum mill, a creamery, a cold storage building, a blacksmith shop, a church, a cemetery, brick kilns and sawmills.

Between 1876 and 1901, the Strasburg School was built at Dunbar Road, west of Keegan Road. It ran until 1946 and today is a private residence. The Strasburg Evangelical Church was established in 1871 and rebuilt in 1888 by the Strasburg Station.

The Immanuel Lutheran Church and cemetery were built on Saum Road east of Strasburg Road, from 1849 to 1866. The cemetery was sometimes called the Ida East Cemetery. In the 1830s, a cholera epidemic swept

Strasburg today. *Author.*

through Monroe County, and many of the church's parishioners died from the disease. They were buried in the church cemetery. When a new cemetery site was chosen, it was decided not to relocate the bodies for fear of disease. The area was abandoned and sold at some point. In the 1920s, the owner of the land discovered some tombstones as he was plowing and brought them to the new cemetery. The bodies remained where they were originally buried, however. Today, all that remains are two large boulders with plaques on them. One denotes the site of the former church and cemetery, and the other has the names and birth and death dates of the forty-eight people who were formerly buried there and, lest we forget, still remain.

Cholera had a devasting effect on Strasburg. A whole family was wiped out in just twenty-four hours. There were no services. Neighbors hurriedly made boxes, and the family members were buried in their own yard. The only thing indicating a graveyard was there was a rail fence, which has since long disappeared. Everyone was afraid to have anything to do with the remains lest they catch the dreaded disease themselves.

Industry was very much alive in the village. James Mills ran a very successful sawmill. He specialized in cutting wood to order. The

Strasburg today. *Author.*

Weipert & Meyer delivery wagon, Strasburg. *Monroe County Library System, Ellis.*

farmers would come to the mill with their own wood and specify what measurements they wanted it cut down to. Two customers named Weipert and Hansberger kept bringing in large lots of walnut logs to have them cut. James would charge four dollars per thousand feet. James also purchased trees on peoples' farms for eight dollars per thousand feet and would cut and sell the wood himself.

One L.W. Newcomber built a cold storage building and paid residents to help bring ice up from the River Raisin. He bought local farmers' eggs and stored them in the building. He also constructed the first general store in Strasburg, later selling it to Will Weipert and Will Knapp. Still later, they sold it to C.W. Rau, who ended up opening the town's post office, express office and freight office in the store. But Weipert decided he wanted back in business and, with the help of Jacob Meyer, opened a rival general store right across the street.

John Dusing had a sorghum mill one mile east of Strasburg. There was also a brick kiln owned by the Wittenburgers. The water for the kiln came from one of the numerous artesian wells throughout the area.

Today, little remains of Strasburg but a couple buildings and houses. Even the railroad tracks are no longer there. Strasburg shows up on the 1876 Beers atlas up through the 1970s, on other maps under Raisinville and Ida.

Taylorsville (North Raisinville)

Taylorsville was named for Amos P. Taylor, who founded the settlement in the early 1800s along with Elephalet Clark. Taylor became the first postmaster of the new post office on March 6, 1833. Later, on January 20, 1838, the post office was renamed North Raisinville and finally closed on March 19, 1879.

The area shows up on the 1859 Geil map on Barnaby property and by lime kilns. It also appears on 1873 and 1909 Monroe County maps.

Chapter 16

SUMMERFIELD TOWNSHIP

Bateman

The name Bateman shows up in a few different places, but little is known about this hamlet. East Batman is mentioned as a place in the June 10, 1921, edition of the *Monroe Evening News*.

Logan Valley

Not much is known about the settlement of Logan Valley. It was named after Josiah Logan. According to the 1876 Beers atlas, a lot of Logans owned property in the area, near the border of Lenawee County in Summerfield Township. On Ida-Center Road, between Robinson and Lenawee County Line Roads, there is the small Logan Valley Cemetery, established in 1896. There was also a Logan Valley School, located on Ida-Center Road; its name was changed to Logan in 1932, and it closed in 1954.

In the vicinity of this area, a bootlegging incident was reported on July 24, 1925. State police officers were tipped off about illegal bootlegging activity involving some Toledo residents who were making numerous trips back and forth to the Petersburg area. The police staked out the area for more than a week. Finally, they encountered the Reo speed wagon the men were reported to be using. They caught up with the car and ordered the two men to stop. Instead, the car sped off at sixty miles per hour with the officers in hot pursuit. After trying to pass the bootleggers and pressing on the horn trying to get them to pull over, the policemen resorted to their guns and opened fire. They managed to hit a tire, which slowed the car to forty. The officers kept firing, peppering the rear tires with holes and finally forcing the criminals to stop. The officers placed the two men under arrest and quickly discovered the contraband inside flowing out all over the car from the bullet-laden containers. It turned out that there was 250 gallons of moonshine whiskey stowed in the car. The hootch was seized and the men brought to the jail in Monroe. One of the men pleaded guilty, while the other pleaded innocent. Both were released on bond.

Chapter 17

WHITEFORD TOWNSHIP

Berringer's Corners (Bearinger's Corners, Robideaux's Corners)

Berringer's Corners was located at Sylvania Petersburg Road and Samaria Road. There were two stores located at the corner: one owned by Forrest Eighemy that was a traditional general store, and the other by Redlinger's.

Unfortunately, the area is best known for a tragic event that took place there. In June 1920, the Robideaux Wesleyan Church became a chaotic scene of murder instead of peace. It all started when the Reverend Louis J. King started preaching there. Apparently, he held a weeklong revival in which he made disparaging comments about other denominations. He was known previously to have published anti-Catholic periodicals before he came to the church. King, a Toledo resident, was a former Catholic himself.

The revival spurred a lot of unrest, and the police were called multiple times to try to maintain control. They deputized several locals to assist, and Michigan state troopers were also called in. As the week went on, word got out about what was going on, and some of the members of St. Joseph Catholic Church in Erie as well as the locals went to listen for themselves. Unfortunately, the result was chaos. Multiple versions of the events that night were brought out in the trial. We may never know exactly what happened.

Late at night, around ten o'clock, on June 27, 1920, three cars full of locals came to the church and stormed in shouting at Reverend King. Even though the deputies demanded that the men leave, most did not. Walter

Berringer's Corners today. *Author.*

Gilday, his brother Byron Gilday and Maurice Drouillard, all members of St. Joseph's, stayed in their car waiting. Walter was a former deputy sheriff, and Drouillard owned the Erie Hotel. Around one o'clock in the morning, people started coming out of the church. At some point, shots suddenly rang out and hit the car the men were waiting in. Walter was killed instantly, and Drouillard was mortally wounded, dying a few days later.

This is where things get really muddled. Deputies say one of the cars headed in the direction of the congregation; Byron Gilday, who survived, said their car never moved. Oddly enough, the very next day, one of the recently deputized citizens, Albert Sherman, a farmer from Summerfield Township, gave himself up to police. He claimed that he was fired on by someone in a car and fired back in self-defense.

Judge Jesse H. Root presided over the Albert Sherman murder trial, in which Sherman was accused of killing Walter Gilday. During arguments, eyewitnesses for the state claimed that the men in the car had no weapons. But the defense alleged that Sherman only shot back in self-defense because he was fired at first. Albert Sherman was found not guilty. He returned to his occupation of farming and died at eighty years old.

Walter Gilday was about thirty years old when he died instantly from the bullet that went through his chest and spine. He was buried at St. Joseph's Cemetery in Erie.

Maurice Drouillard was forty years old when he sustained the gunshot wound to his spine. He was a father of four and on his deathbed still maintained that no one in the cars from Erie that night had any weapons. He was buried in St. Joseph's Cemetery in Erie as well.

Reverend King was told not to return to Monroe County, but he continued to preach in Ohio. Eventually, he was arrested and sentenced to prison for disturbing the peace. He died at age eighty-two in Toledo.

News of the church riot and subsequent murders spread like wildfire and the community was rocked to its core. Eventually, the church was torn down, and slowly, peace returned to the residents of Berringer's Corner.

The area shows up on the 1859 Geil map, and on the 1901 Lang map the name Robideaux and stores show up on parcel no. 10.

GERT

Gert was a small village that grew up along the intersection of Sylvania-Petersburg and School Roads. It had its own post office from February 16, 1895, until March 31, 1904, with John Gilhouse as postmaster. Gert was named after Gilhouse's daughter, Gertrude.

The post office was located inside Gilhouse's general store. He also had a cheese factory. The store was also called Gert's Store and was at the corner

Former Gert store and post office today. *Author.*

of Sylvania-Petersburg Road and School Road. The cheese factory was at Gilhouse's farm. The Gert School shows up on the 1859 Geil map at Samaria and Sylvania-Petersburg Roads. It was rebuilt in 1898 in the same location and changed its name in 1932 to Ferris School. It closed in 1959 and was sold at auction in 1961 and torn down shortly after.

Today, the general store can still be seen but as a repurposed duplex. Gert shows up on the 1859 Geil map up through 1930 on other maps.

Hawthorne

Hawthorne was a station on the Toledo and Ann Arbor Railroad in 1878. There is a Hawthorne Road by Ottawa Lake. There was a post office from 1878 where the tracks crossed Dean Road. Otherwise, little is known about this village.

Ottawa Lake

Ottawa Lake is named after the lake next to it. This area was the first in Whiteford Township to lure settlers. Settlers came to the area in the early 1830s, and it became a station on the state's first railroad line, the Erie and Kalamazoo Railroad, in 1834. Later, the railroad became the Lake Shore and Michigan Southern Railroad and was nicknamed the Old Road. A post office was put in on June 12, 1846, with John Wilder as the first postmaster. He donated the land for the post office. Part of the land for the railroad depot was donated by him as well. The other part was leased from William Bell for ninety-nine years. The street the depot was on became known as Railroad Street. The depot caught fire twice in its existence. The second time, on September 10, 1956, it threatened the whole village of Ottawa Lake as high winds carried embers into the town. The Ottawa Lake Missionary Chapel caught fire but was quickly extinguished; the depot was a total loss, however.

Postmaster Wilder also ran a grocery store and drugstore located in his home, which was between Brown and Railroad Streets. Up until 1944, the post office was always located in the place of business of its postmaster. In 1944, it finally got a building of its own, at Brown and Railroad Streets. The unincorporated community of Ottawa Lake still has its own post office today.

In its history, the post office was broken into four times. The first time was in 1950, when two well-known criminals, the Russell brothers, broke in by sliding down the coal chute. Although they were unsuccessful in stealing any valuables, they did cause a lot of damage to the safe. In 1955, the post office was broken into again; the robbers cut out the glass in the front door to gain access. Then two years later, in 1957, it was broken into yet again.

The most memorable robbery occurred in 1965, however, when two thieves were thwarted by state police troopers. Troopers Dwayne Wheat and Wilbur Rykert noticed a man in the building at two thirty in the morning as they were patrolling the village. Trooper Wheat went around to the back of the building, where he came upon one of the robbers, who fired at him, telling him not to come any closer. Wheat ducked behind the building and yelled to his partner to radio for backup. Suddenly, another shot was fired as the two robbers fled from behind the building to a car. They sped off, and the search was on, but the robbers were not caught. In the post office, they'd managed to damage the safe's combination lock, but before they could grab the loot in the vault, they were spotted by the troopers. In their haste to leave, they left tools and eight sticks of dynamite behind. They had gained entry through a bathroom window. Mr. and Mrs. Don Kathern, who lived above their hardware store next to the post office, overheard the men outside saying they had better get out of there since the police were radioing for help.

Ottawa Lake School shows up on the 1859 Geil map and the 1876 Atlas, at the junction of US 23 and Clark Road on land belonging to J. Wilder. It was a wooden-framed building and is believed to possibly have been a house. It was called the US 223 Schoolhouse and then Montgomery School. In 1898, a new brick structure was built at Brown Street in the village. In 1929, yet another schoolhouse was built behind it, and the one from 1898 was demolished. The new one ran until 1968, and then two years later, it was auctioned off.

St. Michael's Lutheran Church of Ottawa Lake was organized in 1867, but the church was not built until 1888. The Church of Christ was built on Brown Street in 1898 on land donated by Christian Stout. The brick came from the Stout Brick Yard just north of the village. The Church of God was also built on Brown Street just before the turn of the century. The 1876 Beers atlas shows that the area belonged to Dewey-Warren Stave Company, which was owned by Christian Stout in the early 1890s. Zion Church started on October 6, 1861, with a new constitution; the building was finished in 1865 on land donated by Lewis Wasman on Ottawa Lake Road. The

Above: Former Ottawa Lake Church today. *Author.*

Opposite: Ottawa Lake Cemetery. *Author.*

church caught on fire on December 31, 1910, and was rebuilt larger than the original. But only five years later, in August 1915, it caught fire again when it was struck by lightning and was a total loss. The church was rebuilt yet again, this time on property belonging to John Wilder. Another church, Mission Baptista Church of Ottawa Lake, was located in a former post office at the corner of Brown and Railroad Streets.

The Ottawa Lake Cemetery (Lakeview) has graves going back to 1831 and is probably the oldest in the township of Whiteford. It is bounded by M-151, Head-O-Lake and Cemetery Roads. The Legacy Golf Course in Whiteford Township is not your average run-of-the mill golf course. Wander to the sixteenth hole by Noble's Pond, and in contrast to the manicured beauty of the lawn and trees, you will see broken-up tombstones where a cemetery still exists. Thus far, two burials by the pond have been confirmed; investigation is still ongoing. The private cemetery was once known as the Noble's Pond Cemetery.

As early as 1834, General David White built the first sawmill on ten-mile creek. By the 1860s, Ottawa Lake was quite the boomtown, and by the

1880s, it was considered an industrial center. It had numerous sawmills, a stave factory and stave sheds, a lath mill, brick, lime and tile kilns; numerous grocery stores; saloons; a buggy and carriage factory; a casket factory; a depot; a post office; a school; a parochial school; a boardinghouse; factory houses; blacksmiths and many churches.

Lime kilns were running as early as 1838 in the area. There were five lime kilns in Ottawa Lake that generated 2,500 bushels a year. Christian Stout ran a tile and brick kiln and even had a boardinghouse with twenty-eight rooms for his workers, but it was only for those who were single. Anthony Bordeaux ran a boardinghouse just outside Ottawa Lake on the Toledo-Adrian Road; he also owned a blacksmith shop and a wagon shop in the village. One A. Jones did general blacksmithing and horseshoeing and made iron parts. John J. Schnetzler came to the area in 1882 and was a foreman for the Dewey Warren Stave Company. There was even a butchering business, run by Higby, Roberts and Company in 1870s, then by Danny Bay in the 1920s.

In the 1870s–80s, sawmills dotted farmers' property everywhere: William Bell, Lewis Bunge, Samuel H. Jones, L. Knoblauch, D. Johnston and George Hiram Hubbard all had sawmills. George Hinds had a sawmill but also specialized in manufacturing broom handles and other wooden items. The largest sawmill was Dewey-Warren Company, in conjunction with the stave factory in the village. There were four employees working there in 1880: Phillip Perry Jr., John Murphy, Dolpheus DeCant and Isadore DeCant. Sixty-eight-year-old Samuel Van Tassel was the night watchman. The company had two factories, as well as places for the employees to live, a company store with a post office and, possibly, a saloon. Unfortunately for the men, employee safety was not thought of much back then, and many a man lost fingers while working in the mills. At its peak, the mill employed forty to fifty people.

Heirs of Christian Stout started a flour mill in 1898, and it eventually grew into a grain elevator known as the Ottawa Lake Co-op Elevator Company. They bought and sold grains and other items, besides just grinding them. The mill was mortgaged, and the first owner was J. Edward Dawson. Over the years, it was bought out numerous times.

Warren ran not only a stave and heading mill but also a general store, and when residents brought him wood for his mill, he bartered with them, and they received goods in exchange. The wood for the mill was mostly elm, maple or ash. It was characterized as bolts. A three-foot tree trunk was considered a stove bolt. A heading bolt was two feet long. The wood was steamed in big vats. After that, it was split and shaved down to the desired size. It was then shipped out of town to barrel makers. The mill closed in the early 1890s, but not before leaving the surrounding—previously heavily wooded—area looking like a prairie.

Before Ottawa Lake was a village, it was the site of many Native American gatherings. Numerous Native artifacts found in the area attest to this. In the middle of the lake was Plum Island, where an old legend says that a Native American buried gold—but after he buried it, he was never seen again, and neither was the gold.

Ezra Daniels, who was born in New York in 1847, came to the area with his parents and in 1872 purchased the Ottawa Lake Quarry. He employed two men and managed to produce three hundred to five hundred cords a year of building stone. Thus, at the turn of the twentieth century, Ottawa Lake itself was actually a sink or hole two miles long and narrow, except for one point where it was about half a mile wide. Each season, it would fill with water teaming with fish. But usually by November it had evaporated, with much of its water seeping through the rock beneath. Rumor had it that at the foot of the lake, there was a large cave in the rock that was explored up to fourteen feet of depth at some point in the past. Yet subsequent searches yielded different results. All that was found was a sixteen-foot-wide opening in the mud, about five feet deep.

Quarries were abundant in this area. There was the Big Sink (Ottawa Lake Quarry), and the Little Sink or Cummins Quarry at Halfway Creek, founded in 1865 by Morris Cummins. For a while, around 1900, the quarrying of soil was attempted at the Big Sink, located at the intersection of Rauch and Summerfield Roads. Soil was cut and rolled up and allowed to dry in the sun to be used as fuel. Unfortunately for the owners, a Mr. Zamore and the Seyfang Bakery of Toledo, the attempt was not successful.

The first quarter of the twentieth century saw a shift in Ottawa Lake, from an industrial hub to a business hub centered on merchants. Grocery stores, garages, a grain elevator, confectionaries, saloons, hardware stores, a bank, a depot, a post office, a movie theater, a chicken hatchery and more continued to lure people to the area. A 1921 pocket directory listed eighteen stops that were only a few miles away on the Toledo and Western line. David Guestwright had a barbershop and confectionary store, Christ Gerber had a meat market, Charles Kading ran a grocery store and Kuhlman ran a grocery store with harness shop. Earl Fox ran a grocery store that carried dry goods, shoes and boots. It was robbed a couple times, with all the merchandise stolen, yet it managed to remain open until the 1950s, with numerous owners. There were also many saloons, such as "Cap" Morisse's Saloon. Fred Wahl Sr. had a popular saloon that did a booming business during Prohibition, since Ohio became a dry state before Michigan. Ohioans crossed the state line and purchased hootch by the suitcase-full—literally, they would take their contraband back across the state line in suitcases. George Poulous opened a confectionary store at 8440 Brown Street, but over the years, the building changed owners and businesses. It was probably best known as Stout's Tavern, opened by Waid Stout in 1932. In 1942, it became Clark's Tavern, owned by Myrtle Clark; over the years it changed hands and finally caught fire in 1971.

In 1915, a bank was started in the back of James White's grocery store called the People's Bank of Rothfuss Brothers & Company of Ottawa Lake,

Bank and post office, Ottawa Lake, built in 1916. *Monroe Publishing Company.*

Michigan. In the early 1900s, White served as justice of the peace, township clerk and Whitefield township treasurer. Within a year, a brick bank building was built at Brown and Railroad Streets. It was very impressive, with high ceilings, a large vault and barred teller windows. The bank had already been robbed once, when it was in the general store, of $1,400. But it proved to be too much of a temptation and was robbed for a third time on December 20, 1919, in the morning. Six armed men entered the bank and ordered everyone to put their hands up, but the cashier ducked behind the counter. One robber shot at him right through the panel and hit him in the leg. The bullet went straight through. The robbers tied him up along with the bookkeeper and a customer and threw them in the vault, locking the steel door behind them. Now they could flee with their bounty:

$400 in cash and $3,000 in Liberty bonds. They ran through the bank to a car waiting outside for them. The three men trapped in the vault were able to secure their freedom with a screwdriver and a hatchet. Later, it was learned that the robbers fled to Holland, Ohio, where they continued their crime spree. They nabbed a man named Robert Gibson and forced him to drive them in his own car to the fringes of Toledo, where they kicked him out and stole his car. The case was never solved, but the bank in Ottawa Lake became famous through stories of the robbers being the infamous gangsters Al Capone and Cowboy Hill.

Today, it is hard to imagine all the industry and mercantile businesses at Ottawa Lake; there are golf courses, a post office, a church, a cemetery and a store or two. The once bustling, booming community is a quiet, peaceful, slow-paced area now.

Ottawa Lake shows up on the 1859 Geil map and on up to 1972 in other maps under Lambertville.

Pleasant View

Pleasant View exists as a cemetery today at 9704 Head-O-Lake Road, Ottawa Lake. It shares the name with the Lakeview Cemetery, they are one in the same cemetery. The oldest section dates all the way back to 1831. Sometime around 1876 or so, a settlement grew up along the Toledo, Ann Arbor and North Michigan Railway line. Unfortunately, little more is known about Pleasant View.

The area shows up on the 1876 Beers atlas.

Saint Anthony

A settlement grew up around the St. Anthony Roman Catholic Church—started in 1907 and completed about a year later—mostly because of its location midway between Ottawa Lake and Temperance, on the south side of M-151 between Summerfield and Whiteford Roads. Reverend Dennis Needham was the first pastor, and there were eighty-seven families in the congregation in 1907.

The Detroit, Toledo and Ironton Railroad passed through the hamlet crossing M-151 and running north to south. It appears that it went through the area six times a day. It was often called the Ragweed Special.

St. Anthony Church. *Author.*

In 1876, there were three blacksmiths in the settlement, and they made wagons and carriages to order. Hank Homeier ran a store there in the early 1900s. The Harbauer Company of Toledo, Ohio, built forty large vats in a shed behind Hank's store for pickle grading. Here, the pickles would be dipped out of the vats, loaded onto railroad cars and taken to a plant on Detroit Avenue for processing. The soil in this area was sandy and good for produce. Pickles, tomatoes and sugar beets were grown. The tomatoes were taken to a station in the village of Ottawa Lake, and the sugar beets were delivered by truck each fall to the Northern Ohio Sugar Company of Findley, Ohio, which opened in 1955. Orchards were another common sight in the area.

Today, there is little left but the St. Anthony Church and some homes. The area shows up on a 1930 map.

Seeley District

Seeley District was located on the corner of Clark and Yankee Roads on land belonging to General David White. In 1834, General White brought some property and later sold it to Samuel F. and his wife A.M. Seeley. In 1849, they sold off a little of the property for a school at Yankee and Clark Roads. The Seeley School opened in 1849 and was enlarged and rebuilt with brick in 1864. It ran until 1920, when it was hit by a terrible tornado that also destroyed other buildings. It was rebuilt yet again, out of wood this time, and was used until 1959. In 1961, it was sold at auction. Since then, it has been torn down.

Seeley appears on the 1859 Geil map on parcel no. 31. There is also a blacksmith shop and the notation "s.f."; there is no explanation on the map for this notation, however.

UNNAMED VILLAGE

At the corner of Hicker and Yankee Roads existed a village that apparently was not named, or the name was never recorded. It had a blacksmith shop, a cooper shop and some homes in 1850.

WHITEFORD CENTRE

One of the township's earliest inhabitants, and the most noteworthy, is its founding father, General David White, after whom the township Whiteford and the town Whiteford Centre were named. It is thought (although unconfirmed) that he originally migrated from Massachusetts and fought in the War of 1812, where he received the rank of general. He was the first supervisor of Whiteford Township.

Whiteford Centre was called "a smart village" in 1840 by traveler Elmwood Comfort. At some point in its past, it was called Bugtown, possibly, because of all the lightning bugs that called it home.

A log schoolhouse was built at the intersection of Whiteford Centre and Temperance Roads in 1852. In 1856, a new wooden one was built; it was used until 1888, when another, larger brick building was constructed. It was open until 1959. Today, it is preserved as the Little Red Schoolhouse Museum.

There were three churches in Whiteford Centre. The Free Methodist Church was one of the first churches built, on West Temperance Road near Whiteford Center Road. St. Michael's Lutheran Church was built in 1888 on a lot bought for fifty dollars. The Whiteford Centre Congressional Church was built in 1902.

Former little red schoolhouse today. *Author.*

The village got a post office, Whiteford Centre, on June 26, 1867. In 1893, the spelling of Centre was changed to Center. The post office ran until September 30, 1905, with Hiram Wakeley as the first postmaster; he served until 1886. Wakeley was born in 1815 in Albany, New York, and originally settled in Ohio for twelve years, then moved to Whiteford Centre. He was a farmer and a shoemaker and opened the village's first grocery store in 1866; the post office was in his store. The store was located at the northwest corner of Whiteford Center and West Temperance Roads. Wakeley was elected supervisor of Whiteford township in 1854; he served until 1862 and was reelected many times. In 1861, he was also a United States marshal during the Civil War.

The village also had three general stores, owned by Hiram Wakeley, Worter Shaffer and Jacob Slick. Wakeley's, run by brother and sister Ed and Myra Wakeley, was a casket-making shop first, then a barbershop and many other things before it was a general store. In 1876, G.M. Ward operated a grocery store on Whiteford Center Road across from the school.

Jacob L. Slick, who also owned a general store, was born in 1842 and, while fighting in the Civil War, became a prisoner of war at the Battle of

Athens, Alabama, in 1864. After the war, April 27, 1865, he boarded the 260-foot wooden steamboat *Sultana* at Memphis, Tennessee, headed for home. He was among 2,000 soldiers on a ship that was only supposed to carry 376. But the soldiers were not concerned about numbers, nor did they know that the steamer had suffered a boiler problem just four days earlier. On a tight schedule and eager for an army contract, the captain had the boilers patched temporarily and decided to make one trip with all the soldiers instead of two trips.

But not long into the journey, the ship was struggling against the strong current of the spring thaw, and with all the extra weight, the boilers could no longer handle the pressure. Suddenly, they burst into a huge explosion, spitting fire and smoke high up into the air and leaving a gaping hole in the ship. Most of the soldiers did not know what hit them. Those who survived swam desperately toward shore, but most did not make it. Later, 200 men would succumb to their injuries after surviving the ordeal. In all, out of 2,000 men, only 200 survived; 1,800 perished. The *Sultana* would forever be known as the "deadliest maritime disaster in U.S. history—worse than the *Titanic*," according to *Smithsonian Magazine*. Out of those from Monroe, about 36 percent perished, but luckily for Jacob Slick, he was not one of them, and he settled in Whiteford Centre in 1885 and opened his store. A year later, he was made postmaster.

Charles Mallet built a steam-powered sawmill just south of the village, and he employed a number of men. The mill burned down at some point, but he rebuilt it. Isaac J. Ordiway bought the Mallett Sawmill in 1880. He was a successful businessman, manufacturing all kinds of variations of lumber.

Henry N. Paquett was born in Vienna in 1857 and in 1881 settled in Whiteford Centre as a blacksmith; he also served as a constable. Jack Spriggs and H.L. VanOrman also ran blacksmith shops. Sam McMicken (McMeekin) and Marsellus Salute were bootmakers. George Frent operated a cooper shop that employed seven workers.

In 1924, Sheeley's store opened just south of Whiteford Center and was a store in the true sense of the word, offering everything from sacks of flour to Model T parts. Unfortunately, the store was robbed so many times that Sheeley was finally forced to close.

The village had its share of tragedies as well. At the time of the Great Chicago Fire of 1871, Whiteford Centre was going through its own great fire, which started on the outskirts of the village. But the high winds served to fan the flames into the village for a long distance.

Lake Shore and Michigan Southern Railroad, Monroe. *Monroe Publishing Company.*

Another unfortunate event occurred when a settler murdered his mother-in-law. He was sentenced to life in prison, where he invented a shell skein for wagons—a metal band put on the wooden axle-arm to help prevent the wood from wearing rapidly. He obtained a patent and was paid $200; he sent the money to his sons.

Today, the Little Red Schoolhouse Museum can be seen standing almost as a sentinel in a quiet community with little to nothing else but homes and a church. Whiteford Centre appears in the 1876 Beers atlas and other maps up through 1972 under Lambertville.

Chapter 18

OTHER AREAS

CORNERS

The word *corners* was often used to describe a neighborhood where there were crossroads and many members of the same family lived. Some examples are:

Deans Corners

The *Monroe Evening News* reported that around nine o'clock at night on October 27, 1923, there was a barn fire in Dean's Corners. South of Erie, a large barn caught fire and burned to the ground. There were twenty horses in it, and twelve were rescued; the other eight perished. A large quantity of hay and grain was also lost, estimated at $400. The horses were owned by Arnold Construction Company, which was contracted to build the terminal yards of the Pere Marquette Railroad Company.

Delands Corners

Located in the Ottawa Lake area, Delands Corners was mentioned in the *Monroe Evening News* on November 8, 1923. There was a Deland School located at 10250 Summerfield Road.

Dulls Corners

Dulls Corners was mentioned in the *Monroe Commercial* on July 10, 1885, which reported that John Sorter operated a lime kiln thirty rods south of Dulls Corners, one mile west and one mile north of Temperance.

Emerson Corners

The *Monroe Evening News* mentions Emerson Corners in the Steiner area in 1921.

Four Corners

Four Corners was in the southwest corner of Erie Township. There was a post office located on the west side of Dixie Highway just north of Four Corners. Mr. Zimmerman was the blacksmith, and there was also a tavern on one of the corners. Mr. Hall, who lived one block north of Four Corners, was the undertaker for the area, succeeding Mr. Spitter. Spitter was also the postmaster and a cabinetmaker, and he had a shop in the front of his house. The area was mentioned in the *Monroe Evening News* in 1923.

Freys Corners

Freys Corners existed around the turn of the twentieth century in Berlin Township. Members of the Frey family and others settled there. The area was about a mile north of St. Charles Church at the intersection of Dixie Highway, Strong Road and the U.S. turnpike. Some of the earliest residents of the township built beautiful Victorian homes on each corner, such as the Niedermeier, Frey and Barron families.

Ida Corners

In Raisinville Township, in the area of Grape, was Ida's Corners. It was located at the northwest corner of Ida- Maybee and South Custer Roads. It was essentially a store and gas station in the 1920s. The store went through a number of different owners until 1958, when it was torn down for the widening of South Custer Road.

Kelleys Corners/Crossing

Kelley Road exists today in Lasalle, and it can be assumed Kelley was the name of the family in the area.

Knaggs Corners

Knaggs Corners was in Erie Township at the intersection of Bay Creek and Vienna Roads in the 1820s. Evidently, the Knaggs family lived in the area.

Palmers Corners/District

Palmers Corners was located at Palmer Road in Exeter Township. The Palmer School shows up on the 1859 Geil map at Ostrander and Plank Roads. After 1876 but before 1901, the school was rebuilt at the junction of Townsend and Ostrander Roads. It ran until 1948, and today, it is a private residence at 9805 Townsend Road.

Zion Corners (West Zion)

Zion Corners is mentioned in the *Monroe Evening News* in 1921 and 1922 and was in Dundee Township.

OTHER AREAS

Belden: Nothing is known about this hamlet.

Brewer: In Dundee Township, there is a Brewer Road.

Brighton: A village in 1830.

Fork's Switch: In 1864, this was a station on the Lake Shore and Michigan Southern Railroad.

Garrigans: Is mentioned on a 1930 map.

Prentice: A post office was established in 1873 and ran until 1874, with Joseph M. Bale as the first postmaster.

Strong's: An area in Berlin Township where the Strong family owned a lot of property and there was a railroad depot.

Yagerv: The first postmaster in the hamlet of Yagerv was Charles Wilson, in 1895.

BIBLIOGRAPHY

Books

Adams, Donald R. *Bedford Township Monroe County, Michigan: Then and Now*. Temperance, MI: Adams, 2003.

Bidlack, Russell E. *Monroe County History, 1780–1830*. Monroe, MI: County Historical Commission, 1986.

Bulkey, John McClelland. *The History of Monroe County, Michigan: A Narrative Account of Its Historical Progress, Its People, and Its Principal Interests*. Chicago: Lewis, 1913.

Childs, Marion. *Recollections of Life in Monroe County Vol. I & II, 1956–62*. Monroe, MI: Monroe County Library System, n.d.

Fetzer, Madeline Logan. *Voices of Whiteford, Whiteford Township, Michigan*. Toledo: Kahl Brothers, 1976.

Gindy, Gaye E. *The Underground Railroad and Sylvania's Historic Lathrop House*. Bloomington, IN: AuthorHouse, 2008.

Heinlein, Dorothy R., and Martha A. Churchill. *Dundee*. Images of America series. Charleston, SC: Arcadia Publishing, 2011.

Keehn, Shirley, and Frieda Kellie. *The History of Cemeteries and Family Burial Plots in Monroe County, Michigan 1795–2011*. Monroe, MI: Monroe County Historical Commission, June 2005, revised 2011.

LaVoy, Lambert M. *Bay Settlement of Monroe County, Michigan*. Monroe, MI: LaVoy, 1971.

Mazur, Shawna L. *Hidden History of Monroe County, Michigan*. Charleston, SC: The History Press, 2022.

Meints, Graydon M. *Along the Tracks: A Dictionary of Named Places on Michigan Railroads.* Mount Pleasant, MI: Clarke Historical Library, 1987.

Menard, T. Victor. *R.F.D. Newport: A History of Newport and Berlin Township, Michigan.* Monroe, MI: Monroe County Library System, 1995.

Monroe Evening News. *Greetings from Monroe: Historic Postcards of Monroe County, Michigan.* Monroe, MI: Monroe Publishing, 2000.

———. *A Pictorial History of Monroe County, 1876–1941.* Monroe, MI: Monroe Publishing, 1995.

———. *A Pictorial History of Monroe County, 1941–1969.* Monroe, MI: Monroe Publishing, 1996.

———. *Traces of Time: Historic Photos from the Monroe Evening News & Everette Payette Collection, Book One.* Monroe, MI: Monroe Publishing, 2001.

Mull, Carol E. *The Underground Railroad in Michigan.* Jefferson, NC: McFarland, 2010.

Naveaux, Ralph. *Invaded on All Sides: The Story of Michigan's Greatest Battlefield Scene of the Engagements at Frenchtown and the River Raisin in the War of 1812.* Marceline, MO: Walsworth, 2008.

Naveaux, Ralph, and Shana Gruber. *The Floral City: A Brief History of the City & County of Monroe, Michigan, 1830–1930.* Monroe, MI: Monroe County Historical Museum, 2001.

Pageant of Historic Monroe, June 23–24, 1926, Monroe, Michigan. Monroe, MI: Lamour, 1926.

Poupard, Marcel. *Railroad Articles from Monroe County, Michigan.* Self-published, 2009.

Romig, Walter. *Michigan Place Names: The History of the Founding and the Naming of More Than Five Thousand Past and Present Michigan Communities.* Grosse Pointe, MI: Wayne State University Press, 1986.

Siebarth, Jean C. Holtz. *Maybee, Michigan: History of the Village Including Grape, Michigan Area.* Monroe, MI: Kraus Printing, 1998.

Urbani, Trudy Wieske. *Bedford Township.* Images of America series. Charleston, SC: Arcadia Publishing, 2005.

Wing, Talcott Enoch. *History of Monroe County, Michigan.* New York: Munsell, 1890.

Periodicals and Other Publications

Adamich, Tom. "Local History: The Life of Edwin Willits." *Monroe (MI) Evening News*, September 28, 2020.

———. "Monroe County History: Toledo Beach Amusement Park Was Popular Destination." *Monroe (MI) Evening News*, May 15, 2022.

———. "Newport Mills Date Back to 1800s." *Monroe (MI) Evening News*, December 21, 2018.

———. "When Greening's Nursery in Monroe Was a Major Grower." *Monroe (MI) Evening News*, July 28, 2020.

Ainslie, Deliase C. "Village of Brest." Self-published, 1955.

Ann Arbor Michigan State Journal. "Disorder in the Courts." May 7, 1845.

Ann Arbor Register. "Small Pox Outbreak Was Fourteen Cases in Azalia." January 24, 1889.

Capaul, Bill. "Interesting Ida: Lulu-In Ida Township." *Courier & Monroe Ad-Venture*, February 26, 1974.

———. "News from Ida's Past: Federman Is Getting to Be Quite the Town. It Has Two Telephone Lines, Two Railroads, and All That Is Lacking Are the Electric Cars." *Courier & Monroe Ad-Venture*, April 29, 1975.

Churchill, Martha. "Dexter Murder a Family Secret." *Saline Reporter*, June 23, 2011.

———. "When a Milan-Area Family Kept a Dark Secret." *Monroe (MI) Evening News*, August 2, 2020.

Clinton Independent. "Geierman Not Guilty." December 1, 1898.

Cousino, Dean. "There Once Was a Town Named Yargerville." *Monroe (MI) Evening News*, March 21, 1999.

———. "When a 1920 Church Riot in Whiteford Left Two Dead." *Monroe (MI) Evening News*, June 28, 2020.

Detroit News. "More Buried Hamlets Found Near Lost Monroe Village." September 25, 1955.

DeVries, James. "Monroe County Oral History Index." Collection of oral interviews. Monroe Community College and the Monroe County Library System.

Dundee MI Reporter. "Maple Grove." April 30, 1915.

———. "State Police Given Merry Chase Tuesday." July 24, 1925.

Eby, David L. "History of Toledo Beach Amusement Park." *Monroe (MI) Evening News*, October 19, 2020.

Hawkins, Stephanie. "It All Started at Freys Corners." *Monroe (MI) Evening News*, April 25, 2021.

Kisonas, Ray. "Clark City: Only Graves Left." *Monroe (MI) Evening News*, October 27, 1991.

———. "Cone, the Town That Won't Quit." *Monroe (MI) Evening News*, October 10, 1993.

———. "In Monroe's Country Farm Country: Federman Was Travelers Central." *Monroe (MI) Evening News*, March 27, 1994.

———. "Isolation Kept Rea Alive, Good Roads Killed it." *Monroe (MI) Evening News*, November 15, 1992.

———. "Lost Town's Bustle Turns Quiet." *Monroe (MI) Evening News*, June 14, 1992.

———. "On His Account." *Monroe (MI) Evening News*, February 9, 1992.

———. "Sheriff's Office Filled with Stories over 200 Years." *Monroe (MI) Evening News*, August 3, 2017.

Knabenshue, S.S. "The Underground Railroad." *Ohio Archaeological and Historical Publication* 14, no. 3 (1905), 397–400.

LaFaive, Michael D., Patrick Fleenor and Todd Nesbit. "Appendix B: Prohibition in Michigan and the Avenue de Booze," in *Cigarette Taxes and Smuggling: A Statistical Analysis and Historical Review*. Midland, MI: Mackinaw Center for Public Policy, 2008.

Meyers, Arthur V., Gay C. Trace and Robert H. *Trace. Past and Present Country Schools of Monroe County, Michigan.* 1998.

Michigan Daily. "Blacksmith May Plead Guilty To Murder Charge." January 22, 1937.

Michigan Department of Health. *Annual Report of the Commissioner of the Michigan Department of Health*. Vol. 21. Lansing, MI: Robert Smith & Co., State Printers and Binders, 1895.

Monroe (MI) Advocate. "Jobs to Let at Brest." February 14, 1837.

———. "Jobs to Let at Newport." March 28, 1837.

Monroe (MI) Commercial. "Stoney Creek Settlement." April 27, 1876.

———. "Vistula." June 15, 1876.

———. February 17, 1882.

———. February 27, 1885.

———. July 19, 1878.

———. May 4, 1876.

Monroe (MI) Evening News. "Awarded 250." July 15, 1921.

———. "Bullock School." February 23, 1945.

———. "Charged with Still in Auto."" March 18, 1921.

———. "Dean Corners." October 27, 1923.

———. "Dillinger Sought at Beaches Here." March 26, 1934.

———. "Dog's Bark Saves Lulu Post Office Safe and Its Contents of $700." December 8, 1921.

———. "Feds Rule Monroe Plane Crash Resulted in High-Speed Maneuver." December 8, 2012.

———. "Gondola Burns." November 20, 1965.

———. "Injured When Train Strikes Hand Car." February 20, 1917.

———. "Judge Root's Charge to Jury: As Delivered to Jurors in Sherman Murder Case Tuesday Afternoon." January 12, 1921.

———. "Looking Back: Newport Michigan." November 18, 2015.

———. "Loranger Mill Is Damaged." May 24, 1923.

———. "Muehleisen District." October 26, 1922.

———. "New Creamery at Scofield." November 2, 1922.

———. "News Reports Show Monroe Fared Well After Spanish Flu." May 13, 2020.

———. "Old Tavern and Stage Coach Stop," February 19, 1947. Accessed via the Monroe County Library System. https://library. biblioboard.com/content/ebc48194-d0da-41fd-ab4f-f71be14f72ef.

———. "Storekeeper at Scofield Is Dead." September 12, 1923.

———. "Viewed Property." July 14, 1921.

Monroe (MI) Times. "Havre." March 16, 1837.

———. "Havre Branch Rail Road." February 9, 1837.

———. "Havre Branch Railroad Company." May 18, 1837.

———. "Into a Ditch! C.H. & D. Flyer #312 Left the Track Near Flat Creek Culvert Thursday Night. Forty People Hurt. Cause of the Wreck Still a Mystery, Yet Various Opinions Are Expressed." November 16, 1899.

———. March 23, 1837.

———. November 24, 1836.

Philbeam, Byron. "The Way It Was: Rea, Michigan." *Independent*, January 14, 1988.

———. "The Way It Was." *Independent* (Dundee, MI), March 7, 1991, and March 21, 1991.

Potter, Sue. "The Liberty Corners School." *Courier & Monroe Ad-Venture*, August 10, 1971.

Register. "The University Clinic." January 24, 1889.

Roth, Danielle. "Murder at the Dexter Michigan Peninsula Mills Dam." Doctoral thesis, Eastern Michigan University, 2006.

Tanber, George J. "Monroe County: Blink and You'll Miss the Hamlet of Liberty Corners." *Blade*, May 25, 2006.

Toledo (OH) Blade. "2011 Monroe Plane Crash Caused by Pilot Error." December 10, 2012.

Wisler, Suzanne Nolan. "Monroe County's Location Made It a Prohibition Hot Spot." *Monroe (MI) Evening News*, May 28, 2018.

Websites

American Battlefield Trust. "The Sultana Disaster." https://www. battlefields.org/learn/articles/sultana-disaster.

Bartlett, S.M. *County Atlas of Monroe, Michigan, from Recent and Actual Surveys and Records under the Superintendence of S.M. Bartlett for F.W. Beers*. New York: F.W. Beers, 1901. Accessed via the University of Michigan Library. https://quod.lib.umich.edu/m/micounty/3927905.0001.001.

Eschner, Kat. "This Civil War Boat Explosion Killed More People Than the 'Titanic.'" *Smithsonian Magazine*, April 27, 2017. https://www. smithsonianmag.com/smart-news/civil-war-boat-explosion-killed-more-people-titanic-180963008/.

Facebook. "Berlin Charter Township Historical Society." https://www. facebook.com/BerlinTownshipHistory.

———. "Eric Area Historians." https://www.facebook.com/profile. php?id=100080668450266.

———. "Exeter Township Historical Society—Michigan." https://www. facebook.com/exetertownshiphistoricalsociety.

FamilySearch. "Milton Waite." https://ancestors.familysearch.org/en/ L4MM-X8M/milton-waite-1849-1923.

Find a Grave. "Col Norman Jonathan Hall." https://www.findagrave. com/memorial/14259335/norman-jonathan-hall.

———. "Ezra Younglove." https://www.findagrave.com/ memorial/8619268/ezra-younglove.

———. "Hannah B Janney Atkinson." https://www.findagrave.com/ memorial/127760794/hannah-b-atkinson.

———. "Lacey Amasa Atkinson." https://www.findagrave.com/ memorial/130906498/lacey-amasa-atkinson.

———. "Ora Blanche Davis Heath." https://www.findagrave.com/ memorial/5671960/ora-blanche-heath.

———. "Samuel Atkinson." https://www.findagrave.com/ memorial/8890728/samuel-atkinson.

———. "Sayer William Reeves." https://www.findagrave.com/ memorial/60253563/sayer-william-reeves.

Geil and Jones; Worley & Bracher; Geil, Harley & Siverd; and Robert Pearsall Smith. "Map of Monroe County, Michigan." 1859. Library of Congress. https://www.loc.gov/item/2012593018.

Genealogical Society of Monroe County, Michigan. https://gsmcmi.org.

Lang, Geo. E. "Map of Monroe County, Michigan." 1901. Library of Congress. https://www.loc.gov/item/2012593017.

Luna Pier Cook. "Favorite Dive: Chateau Louise, Luna Pier, Michigan." http://micuisine.com/lunapiercook/?p=671.

Macs Motor City Garage. "Henry Ford's Railroad: The Detroit, Toledo & Ironton." https://www.macsmotorcitygarage.com/henry-fords-railroad-the-detroit-toledo-ironton.

Michigan Department of Transportation (MDOT). https://www.michigan.gov/mdot/-/media/Project/Websites/MDOT/Travel/Mobility/Rail/Michigan-Railroad-History.pdf.

Michigan Family History Network. "Michigan Men on the Sultana by Michigan County." http://www.mifamilyhistory.org/civilwar/sultana/countyresults.aspx?County=Monroe.

Michigan One Room Schoolhouse Association. https://www.miorsa.org.

Michigan Railroads. https://michiganrailroads.com.

Michigan State Police. "Trooper Richards F. Hammond." https://www.odmp.org/officer/5994-trooper-richards-f-hammond.

Milan Area Historical Society. http://www.historicmilan.com.

Monroe County Library System. "Havre— Lost Town Built in 1836." Digital collections, local stories. https://monroe.biblioboard.com.

National Archives. "War of 1812 Pension and Bounty Land Warrant Application Files." Accessed via https://www.fold3.com/image/307842470.

99.1 WFMK. "Lulu: A Quaint Little 1853 Village in Monroe County, Michigan." https://99wfmk.com/lulu-michigan.

———. "Pretty Boy Floyds Michigan Hideout." https://99wfmk.com/pretty-boy-floyds-michigan-hideout-1930.

River Raisin National Battlefield Park. "History & Culture." https://www.nps.gov/rira/learn/historyculture/index.htm.

University of Michigan Library. Michigan County Histories and Atlases. *Standard Atlas of Monroe County, Michigan: Including a Plat Book of the Villages, Cities and Townships of the County...Farmers Directory, Reference Business Directory.* Chicago: Geo. A. Ogle, 1896. https://quod.lib.umich.edu/m/micounty/3927818.0001.001

ABOUT THE AUTHOR

Shawna Lynn Mazur was born and has lived in Monroe all her life. She has a bachelor's degree in history and literature. She has had an article published in *Michigan History Magazine* and written a book for the National Park Service, for which she works at River Raisin National Battlefield Park. This is her second book for The History Press; *Hidden History of Monroe County, Michigan* was published in 2022. Shawna lives in Carleton, Michigan, with her husband, Joseph Mazur, and their two dogs, Callie and Cassie.